Backstage

The Importance of Your Personal
Inner Connection

Jan Merendino

i

ALSO BY ELIZABETH JOYCE

Books
Psychic Attack, Are You A Victim?

Ascension—Accessing The Fifth Dimension

Ascension—Accessing The Fifth Dimension Workbook

Opening To Your Intuition and Psychic Sensitivity Developing Your Sixth Sense
BOOK ONE
BOOK TWO and
BOOK THREE

Seeding and Nurturing the Garden of Your Soul

The NEW Spiritual Chakras

Unlimited Realities

MP3 Programs
Spiritual Healing and Meditation
Healing Depression the Natural Way
The Chakras and Your Body
Opening The New Spiritual Chakras
Inserting the Divine Seals
Meditation to Healing From Within

All of the above items are available from
Amazon.com, Ingram, Book Stores, and
Visions of Reality

https://new-visions.com

Backstage

*The Importance of Your Personal
Inner Connection*

By Elizabeth Joyce

Backstage
The Importance of Your Personal Inner Connection

By Elizabeth Joyce

ISBN: 978-0-9972083-5-1

Copyright
April 18, 2020

Cover Artist: Jim Warren
Cover Art Copyright by Jim Warren.
www.jimwarren.com/site/
Email:jim@jimwarren.com

All Bible quotes are from the
King James version (KJV)

Publishing, Editing, and Page Layout by
Visions of Reality
21 Roslyn Ave,
Warner, NH 03278

WEBSITE: new-visions.com
201-934-8986 (24 hr. service)

Printed in the United States of America

DEDICATION

For Pujhita and Sahasha

At radiancehealing.net

and

To anyone who has experienced a serendipity or
cosmic set-up experience and wanted to know why!

TABLE OF CONTENTS

ACKNOWLEDGEMENTS

What I have discovered over the past thirty-three years while sitting at the feet of the Divine Mother, Mata Amritanandamayi, is that through thoughts, devotion, and experience, we can transcend dogma and tradition. She has given to me a new understanding of the evolution of human consciousness and the unlimited opportunities that are with us every moment.

Thank you Alison Reich, Donna Feldhausen, Neal Lorimer, Marie Ann Francouer, Sharon Wyeth, Shiela Leitner, Robert Maldonado, and all of you who have stood by my side in loving friendship, for your unwavering support.

Thank you Christine Shaw for your editing contribution, Mary Carol Sullivan for your graphics, and Jim Warren for your spectacular cover art.

I give special thanks to George Noory. Elizabeth Hepburn, Frank St. James, Sharon Wyeth, Max Wiesen, and Ed Asner for your kindness and belief in my work.

Thank you to every teacher I have met, listened to, meditated with, and grown from your message.

Lastly, I give a heartfelt tribute to Mentor and my invisible teachers backstage. Without you this book could not have been completed.

Backstage

*The Importance of Your Personal
Inner Connection*

By Elizabeth Joyce

INTRODUCTION

"WHAT A COINCIDENCE! " is what we might say when
we run into an old friend we'd just been thinking of.
Is it just a chance encounter—
or is it evidence of something more?

This is the new guideline for spiritual seekers – *the energy
happens before the action.* Those who know they've been
taught half-truths throughout their lifetime now want to
find meaning and add depth to their lives. They're
beginning to realize the energy within them answers this
need.

    One of the most valuable things about learning to
access the *new double helix, fifth dimension energies* is that
it promotes happiness, inner-peace, and wellbeing. By
going within, you can learn pearls of wisdom to guide you
impeccably, and embrace patience, compassion, and
understanding, making your life better today.

    On a personal level, shedding spiritual
misinformation, along with emotional and mental toxicity,
makes you a much Lighter person – happier, more
connected, more compassionate, and a far better wife,

husband, parent, and friend. This powerful, free flowing energy puts you in the flow of great new opportunities, success, abundance, and creative ideas.

What is not known about me is that I was greatly influenced by the understandings and philosophy of the gifts my Grandmother brought into her life. She was a true Shaman and was guided by the followers of the sacred fire. During the year I spent with her as a child, I had thoughts put into my mind while I slept. During times of deep silence I learned about the sacredness of all life and about how to accept things in life without discarding any of it. I am honored with these lessons, and never gave up on finding God in any experience I had in life. For in rejecting any part of God, I was rejecting God entirely.

Now in modern times, people must carefully examine what supported them before and make adjustments and corrections wherever necessary. I wanted to bring my writings to an updated, newer form that would suit this present day reality because of the changing times and planetary shifts. The desire is to bring forth this new understanding to help people remember the *Law of One* and the *Family of God*.

BACKSTAGE raises the question of how we should explain and understand the mysteries in life– with or without a belief in a greater power or meaning to life. Even if every possible coincidence could be scientifically explained, we shouldn't necessarily discount its emotional, energetic, and spiritual impact and importance. You can watch a movie or read a novel, and be at once aware of its non-reality while also being moved by it. Must these feelings and ideas therefore be incompatible? Indeed, might the continued belief in meaningful coincidences even be rational and necessary to our experience of life in the world? Ponder this: perhaps a belief in meaningful coincidences is something vital to our survival as humans.

During the summer of 2018, while on the US Tour with Amma, I requested Her to open my energies to write yet another book to help uplift mankind. She lovingly showed me that we are on the brink of a revolution of consciousness all over the world. The way to move through tough times of darkness and fear is to take the time to connect with your Blessed Higher Self and the Cosmic energies. This is vital if you want to stay balanced, healthy, and productive.

When we experience coincidences, we experience a sequence of events, sometimes perceived to be very rare, are surprising to us, and feel like they are caused by something beyond our knowledge or control. Have you ever had something happen that you just couldn't quite explain? Something you chalked up to *coincidence*? Many people have and some of their stories are in this book. Backstage helps you to understand the *Laws of the Universe, the energy behind them,* and how they work.

The new frequency.

There are a few who carry this frequency that finally arrived on our planet December 21, 2012 from the center of our Milky Way galaxy, unveiling new Spiritual Chakras and Divine Seals. We're now living in a time when Spirit is drawing closer to conscious awareness, a beautiful but confusing part of our evolution. It can feel like distancing from Source as new energy flows through you, because it's so new, yet so powerful.

As you begin to feel and become aware of larger arrays of emotion, new information can clash with your natural, common way of thinking and reacting, destroying and changing your agendas. You begin to think, *What are my true thoughts and feelings?*

Take the time to set up a daily devotional and meditation practice, and Divine Intervention can be activated within you, allowing you to penetrate and access free-flowing energy beyond the astral plane. This will create a space for you to ask that question, and any others you chose – and *listen* to the answers.

Our *being* has many frequencies of aliveness and as we move our attention to the more subtle of these, we discover a portal to the radiant awareness that is always here: the chi, shakti and kundalini. Meditation guides us in using the breath and focused attention as we scan through the body with our mind and third eye to awaken an inner luminosity. We then open our attention to rest within the energetic field of awakened consciousness or awareness.

To harmonize with one's nature or Soul vibration is to become one with the primordial essence of the Universe and merge with those vibrations and frequencies. This invisible energy is metaphysical, as you cannot see, smell, or touch the energy. However, the energy can be "felt" and you become aware of the energy and its essence the more you work with meditation and becoming centered.

This mysterious energy known as Shakti, Chi, or the Holy Ghost, is not a 'name' or a 'thing', but the underlying natural order of the Universe whose ultimate essence is difficult to hold down or understand.

The object of Spiritual practice is to *become One with these energies,* for by whatever name you choose to call them, they are one in the same. This is known as entering into the *State of Being.*

The *philosophy of meditation* is universally the same. Meditation practice is to harmonize with your inner nature in order to achieve that which you have been born to do. Your impact and connection to this energy brings you into a force field containing unlimited possibilities. This energy field has been medically proven to reduce stress, increase happiness and relaxation, increase your sleep time, lower blood pressure, help with depression and bipolar, improve your brain function, and help to reduce pain and anxiety. How you access it and use it is up to each and every individual Soul.

Proper practice variously involves accepting, conforming to, or working with these natural developments.

May this information lead you into the true world of the Soul. Know *that the energy happens before the action.* Many have joined me to tell their stories about coincidence, magical moments, and their realization that there is definitely something tangible beyond the body. Within these pages we learn that the *Spiritual energies* can and do connect with our thoughts and our actions to manifest our desires. *Backstage* explains the principles behind the knowledge, use, and action these invisible energies bring. A belief in meaningful coincidence, from an acting, feeling, living human perspective, is surprisingly rational.

This book is an effort to lay it all out for you to embrace, comprehend, and begin to practice. By learning to meditate, and/or set up a daily practice, you can raise your vibration levels, and reap the benefits of this higher vibratory state, which includes relaxation, moving energy, and opening to a new perspective in your life.

Om, Shanti,Shanti, Shanti

Elizabeth Joyce
February 20, 2019

CHAPTER ONE

WHEN DID IT ALL BEGIN?

Since the first hydrogen bomb was dropped in Japan in 1945, there have been waves of energetic beings in human form brought forth. After 1945 up to 1960 is considered the "first wave" of people carrying the 5ᵗʰ Dimension energies, which are new to this planet Earth.   At this time in the new Millennium of the 2000's, the first wave of people carrying this energy really don't want to be here any longer. They just don't understand the drugs, hatred, war, guns, violence, and all other negative aspects happening on this planet Earth. Sometimes they dwell on their fears, which can cause depression and further emotional concerns.

This powerful energy called *the double-helix of the fifth dimension*, the energies of love, peace, harmony, and brings a higher desire to heal all pain. These first wave beings are actually the leaders of bringing forth a *change in the way of living,* or the activation of a higher consciousness. The first wave of this new form of humans are living their lives, just like everyone else. The difference they bring is kindness, empathy, and the effort to look at the "older" perceptions and apply the metaphysical principles to their lives. They don't participate with the tearing someone down to build themselves up strategy that has been a way of life for centuries. They choose values over money and integrity over cheating and lies.

This first wave of energy awareness humans are finding that they just don't want to be here anymore. They sense this planet has become very dark, very low Third Dimensional, and are feeling stifled from the Light and love of the other, higher dimensions. These Souls just want to go "Home." Many of these Souls want to commit suicide and are having a very difficult time with their day-to-day existence. They have good families, good jobs, are living a comfortable lifestyle, but just do not want to be here any longer.

The second wave, the Souls between their twenties to about age forty-five, are life-giving Souls. They may not have been on this planet before, but heard the call; "Earth is in trouble. Will you go and help?" These Souls can actually attend meetings and refresher courses in another dimension about the assignment they volunteered for and are working on as they walk their path on the planet Earth. In my past life and present life work, I have heard thousands of stories about the lives and the amazing miracles emanating from the positive energies these people carry.

These people are the *antennas* or *generators* of the new, non-judgment love energy of the Fifth Dimension. For example, they can walk through crowds at a mall, enter a sports arena, or go out to dinner at a restaurant and emanate energy that is uplifting and healing to others. Many of these Souls don't like other people because the lower energy vibrations bother them and they are continually fighting off the darkness and re-aligning their energy levels. So they don't go out in public much, and are not completing the task they have set out to do. That is, just to BE.

Many of the first and second wavers never marry, or if they do, choose not to have children. They think that having children creates Karma. They don't want to become entrapped and have to stay here on Earth. Many of them work from home to keep away from other people. These are very gentle and loving people.

The first wavers are having such a difficult time here, but know inside that someone had to begin this ascension process. There had to be a starting point. They began weaving a new life path on Earth, and when the second wave arrived, they could follow the new path already established for them. However, it's difficult cutting through the Maya and creating a higher path to lead mankind into a new life existence.

The third wave are the children of the planet at this writing, many of whom now are in their teens. They began to come along at the end of the 1990's and as we entered the new Millennium. These people are extremely gifted Souls and vibrate way beyond the energies that have been normal for the planet Earth.

These children are the hope of the world as well as a gift to the world. They have incarnated here to really make a difference. These children have come here with all of their elevated DNA, genetics, and gifts from other areas of the Universe. The are familiar with and work with *the New Spiritual Chukras* daily. The last thing they should do is to be put on medication. They truly are a new species, and are here to educate the educators.

Yes – it's certainly true that these children can be very disruptive and appear over-active. The reason for this is that they are bored. A teacher of a math class in junior high school asks the class to find the answer to a problem. Several students raise their hand and say the correct answer. The teacher asks, "How do you know that?" The students respond, "I don't know, I just know." But that's not enough for the teacher because they want the student to break it all down and show how they arrived at the correct answer. To the student, this is ridiculous and a waste of time. They want to move on to more difficult and challenging problems. This exercise is very aggravating to the students.

Teachers tend to go over and over the same material, not realizing that these new students "got it" the first time. This is where boredom sets in. These children need to organize their own group and be given challenging projects that could go beyond that class level. Then they can expand their knowledge and perhaps teach us a few new mathematical truths that we have not yet discovered.

For the younger students, give them something they can take apart and put back together again. This gives them a challenge. My younger son, Jeffrey, who is a second level wave child, exemplified this at the age of four. It was Christmas morning, and the house was full of gifts for the kids. The boys opened their stockings first, as tradition would have it. I had purchased a ten-cent miniature aluminum coffee percolator for him to play with: basically to take apart and put back together again. He was so focused on that small toy that he didn't want to open anything else. He took it apart and put it back together over and over again. Only after he tired of it did he open the other gifts. At that time I did not realize what was going on, but now when I remember that day, I smile with realization of the workings of his mind.

These new children actually have a different way of thinking and grasp things very quickly. They have incarnated to help us evolve with science, math, technology, and in every which way as well. They are a gift to the world.

(NOVA SPECIAL – 10 year olds who have graduated from college and have formed their own organizations.)

There are many new organizations that have been founded having to do with helping the children of the world. They are demonstrating and giving us the gift of community service again, and getting the world back to what it's supposed to be: Heaven on Earth. Through sharing, cooperation, and most of all respect, and by honoring everyone and knowing that we all are born with special gifts, this new world will be created. It's time to be aware of the importance of community sharing as well as time to open our gifts.

Most of the people in this world are caught up in the world of karma and do not have this vision or these gifts. They continue to spin round and round on the wheel of karma. The new waves of human kind are helping to bring this world into new world where we will all have a great time living on the Earth in a wonderful way.

4

We are being led into a direction of ascension, upliftment, and spiritual awareness that will essentially open up to all the parallel worlds and universes for us to share, learn, and grow with as we merge with their energies and knowledge.

This is what is happening Backstage.

Backstage
The Importance of Your Personal
Inner Connection

NOTES:

CHAPTER TWO

MOVING FROM DARKNESS TO LIGHT

Civilization had inherent moral laws since before the time of Abraham. Every culture has its language and laws created by its people. They are to be respected or any offenders would suffer the consequences. However, along with the mores or cultural laws, there are the divine laws. These laws have come down to the Earth plane from a different realm: a higher form of consciousness. They don't necessarily have to be obeyed on Earth, but bring their own set of negative consequences if not applied to life. The result of that, *"those who practice such things will not inherit God's Kingdom"* (Galatians 5:19). As we progress into the third decade of the 21· Century, these Divine Laws seem to be almost obliterated on this planet.

At this time on Earth, reverence seems to have left the planet. Not only in America but other nations as well. Many societies have never heard of the Seven Deadly Sins, much less Spiritual Laws. It all seems to be getting worse. Despite popular culture making light of these sins, they should be taken very seriously. Pride has broken families apart, greed has torn humanity into shreds and envy keeps people from feeling the joy Spirit has provided for each of us. It takes heroic virtue in most cases to overcome these tendencies. Most of us are afflicted greatly with a number of these acts on the list. Once you give into one of these sins, it's so easy for the spirit of the others to come into your heart as well. Thankfully, we have the power to fight the seven deadly sins and live for God. Be assured that this fight will become brutal over the next ten years or more.

We are facing some very dark times we enter the Transformational Twenties. We have an actual fight on our hands, although our adversaries are invisible. If we want to combat the seven deadly sins, and we must in order to survive, the first thing we have to accept is that we can't have everything. You can work hard, save your money, and even buy many things you desire, but the truth is someone else will always have more to their name. We all know the Joneses. They're the ones who just got back from a two-week trip to Europe dragging suitcases stuffed with souvenirs. They drive their kids to private school in their new car, and every weekend, they head out of town – fashionably dressed – to eat at their favorite restaurants. They always seem to have money to do everything they want to do whenever they want to do it. No budget. No worries. They've got it all or so it seems. The truth is, they don't have everything and keeping up with Joneses is not going to bring joy.

God tells us in 1 Corinthians 13:5 that *"love is never jealous," and "loving our neighbors like ourselves"* is something we are called by God to do. The next time you begin feeling envious of what others have, take a close look at what God has blessed you with and say a short prayer of thanks and gratitude. Ask God to bring you the Light, His loving energy, to change your heart and allow you to be grateful for the blessings He has bestowed upon you. Also, pray for the security that God brings to help and guide you along your journey in life. Call in your Spirit Guides and Angels to help strengthen you. The more you feel content and joyful, the less you'll want to stray into the path of temptation. You'll be too busy and fulfilled to do so.

The next thing we have to remember is that life isn't just about us. Your actions and priorities do affect those around you. With that in mind, know that every time you *choose* to be lazy instead of meeting friends you made plans with weeks in advance you're hurting your relationship with them. When you choose to stay in your pajamas, eating, playing games on the computer, or watching movies all day, your relationships suffer, as does your waistline, not to mention your self-esteem. Being lazy doesn't necessarily limit itself to refusing to attend social functions. Being lazy includes the refusal to listen when your inner Spirit Guide tells you to take a few hours each week to help feed the hungry or go to the bank to get some cash to donate to a good cause. It's important that you keep yourself mentally and physically active by participating in community events. Pray for people near and dear to you in your spare time, as well as those throughout the world. Pray for world and universal peace. It makes a dent into the surface of this planet and the energy carries out into the universe as well. When you are doing service, God's work of helping others, you are keeping yourself from allowing the sin of Sloth to overcome you.

Thirdly, we need to make God the most important part of our day. If you're struggling with any of the deadly sins, it's important that you meditate and bring in those essential life-force energies everyday. Communication with Spirit and your Inner Guides is key to your health, wealth, and survival. It's easy to cast this aside, or to tell ourselves, "I'll spend time with God after I do this other thing." Many things seem more urgent and while they may be at the top of your priority list, they are not more important than your Spiritual connection. Spending time with your Spirit Guide and the God force energies is the single-most important priority you'll do each day. Your time reading Scriptures and prayer-meditation should have as its goal a growing love for God. Blissfully, it takes such little effort, and the rewards are more than great.

Finally, we need to confess our sins immediately. When you do commit one of the seven deadly sins, confess it immediately to your inner self, and then move on. Add to your meditations that you desire to be free of this temptation. The Bible tells us. *"If we confess our sins, He is faithful and righteous to forgive us our sins and to cleanse us from all unrighteousness"* (1 John 1:9). In a very practical sense, God's indignation over your daily sins demonstrates His love for you, along with His fatherly discipline to protect you. Keep short written journals with

9

your Spirit Guides, God, and with others. Don't allow unconfessed sins that you can feel so guilty about to weigh down your life. This will only bring you discomfort and disease. Grace is there for that very reason. Grace allows you to move on. Keep confessing your sins. Seek forgiveness, and inner cleansing daily.

The Bible is clear The Bible is clear that the only sin God will not forgive is that of continued unbelief, because it rejects the only means to obtain forgiveness, the Law and Power of Grace. Today, you are provided with the opportunity for self-examination and renewed repentance. Don't let these sins control your heart.

What are the meanings of the Seven Cardinal Sins? What is called sin is the outer manifestation, either in deed or thought, of psychological deviation and immaturity. In other words, the result of inner distortion produces what is called "sin". The common denominator of any sin is immaturity of the Soul, which makes it incapable of relating, communicating, and loving. In the broadest terms, sin is lack of love. An immature person is never able to love. Anyone in that condition is selfish, egocentric, blind, and cannot understand others. Immaturity means separateness. In separateness, one does not love and is therefore "in sin". Sin, in psychological terms, is neurosis. The only difference between the spiritual and psychological approach is that the spiritual approach puts emphasis on the result, while the psychological approach shows the underlying causes and the different currents and components leading to separateness, neurosis, or sin.

The first cardinal sin is The first cardinal sin is PRIDE. Briefly, pride is always a compensation for feelings of inferiority and inadequacy. That the effects of pride lead to separateness is self-explanatory.

The second cardinal sin is COVETOUSNESS — greed. If you covet something you do not possess you blind yourself, because you believe that having what you want would give you happiness, when, in fact, happiness is an inner state-of-being, which can never be achieved by outer means. You are also blind when you ignore the inner causes of not having what you wish to have.

In your search for self-understanding you will come to realize that whatever you lack in your life, provided your wish for it is a healthy one, is caused by a conflict within you. Such a conflict is your being afraid — perhaps unconsciously — of the very thing you want most. You may feel undeserving. You may have desires and be unaware of many obstacles to their fulfillment. Finally, you may be even unaware of what you really wish for. Under these circumstances, you may envy others and covet what they have, because you cannot resolve your own problems, which keep you from fulfilling yourself. What you covet may be a substitute for your real needs of which you may not even be aware.

Covetousness, as well as pride, separates you from others and from your real Self. Both lead to, and stem from, self-alienation; both are opposites of love, of communication, and of relating to others. These vices do not unite, but set you apart and above, in a special, isolated place you think someone else holds. All this is inner blindness, which leads to outer selfishness and to separateness. When your heart opens to this fact, your unhealthy desires will vanish and will not return unless you "fall from Grace" again.

The third cardinal sin is LUST. Lust is so often misunderstood. It is believed to refer to sexuality, but this is not necessarily so. Now, what does lust mean? It means any kind of passionate desire, whether or not it has to do with sexuality, which is indulged in a spirit of egocentricity or isolation, is the childish attitude of "I want to have, to get," or "I want what I want when I want it, without regard of consequences." This erases a true spirit of mutuality. One may be willing to give, provided one receives what one wants, and yet the basic emphasis is placed subtly on the self, rather than on mutuality. True mutuality is not possible without the capacity to relinquish, and to tolerate not always having one's own way. The maturity to withstand frustration and to relinquish one's will is a prerequisite for true mutuality. One has to *radically release* the inner need for greed. This is not easy, but necessary for Soul growth. When the need to receive is a greedy force that is intrinsically selfish, then one can speak of lust.

Backstage
The Importance of Your Personal
Inner Connection

It is easy to be deceived because the stronger this selfish need exists, the more the person may sacrifice, submit, and be a martyr. All this is an unconscious manipulation in order to get one's own way. Since this tendency is subtle and hidden, and often has nothing to do with sexual passions, it may not be obvious that it's lust. Yet all human beings have some of it. Where there is a forcing current and a driving need, there is lust. You all have that, and it is even stronger when it is not yet consciously experienced. You may deceive yourself because that which you so strenuously desire may in itself be something constructive. Yet, you are the craving, needy child who wants to be the center of the universe. *The raging need*, which you may or may not be conscious of, is disconnected from the causes that brought about the original unfulfillment. In your ignorance, the need, desire, or lust swells to unbearable proportions and you become more frustrated because you do not see the remedy, which is always a change of inner direction.

In other words, an unfulfilled need that remains unrecognized in its primary, original form, produces lust. This need could arise from your present life or a past life unfulfillment. To the degree that you become aware of your real needs, you automatically increase your maturity, and lessen the intensity of the desire. When a need is unconscious, a displacement occurs and a substitute need is pursued lustfully. No matter how legitimate, constructive, or rational the desire may be in itself, such a pursuit indicates immaturity. The stronger the urgency, the greater the frustration must be. It does not matter whether this refers to sexual desire, or the lust for power, for money, for being liked, or for a particular achievement or thing. When these emotions are investigated and the original need found, you can begin to dissolve the lust. You can come to terms with the original need, but you never can with the substitute need. If this original need is still childish and destructive, it can mature only by bringing it out into the open. A conscious need can mature into a mutual state where two people recognize and express their own respective needs in such a way as to help each other find

12

fulfillment. An unconscious need will always be one-sided and selfish.

To assume that the sexual urge per se is sinful lust is utter nonsense. Sexuality is a natural, healthy instinct. If it matures properly, it combines with mutuality and leads to love and union. Some of the deepest love can be felt between lovers when one's sexual union is joined up with mutual love and respect for your partner. This is what God intended, not just a physical act, but a joining of the hearts into the oneness of the moment. If this desire remains separate, it is lust. However, it is no more evil than the lust for power, for money, for fame, for always being right, or for anything else.

The fourth cardinal sin is ANGER. What is anger? Anger is always, in a sense, a lie. The original feeling is often one of hurt. If you owned up to the original feeling, you would not need to be angry. When you are angry you are angry with yourself. In pride, due to inferiority, you feel humiliated when you are hurt because you gave someone else the power to hurt you. Therefore, you substitute anger for the original pain. Anger seems less shameful, setting you above the other person, rather than feeling your vulnerability, which seems to be an inferior place. Anger lifts you above the true position you find yourself in: that of being hurt. In pride, you lie about your real feelings. Thus, anger and pride are connected. The lie is one of self-deception and therefore of self-alienation. It is displacement. Thus, this inner lie causes negative effects, while owning up to your feelings does not. Owning up to your error or mistake frees you from guilt, anger, and unhealthy regrets.

Being hurt, but free from anger, cannot negatively affect others; therefore it will not come back to the self. If the primary emotion, pain, or hurt is no longer conscious, or if it is intermingled with the secondary emotion of anger, it turns destructive. Whether the anger manifests in deeds or words, or whether it is merely an emanation; makes no difference. When you admit that you feel hurt, you do not cut off the bridge to the other person; in anger, you do. The genuine, primary emotion is not contrary to love and communication, while the substitute emotion of anger is. I usually shy away from the word "sin" because it

encourages self-destructive and unproductive guilt. Instead I concentrate on the underlying conditions. However, in this context, I have to use this word. Anger which leads away from communication, from bridging gaps between human beings, is a sin. Of course, there is such a thing as healthy anger, but we are not talking about that. There really should be another word for it.

Why is it that in the Bhagavad Gita anger is considered the worst sin of all, producing complete confusion? Because in anger, when it is a secondary reaction, you no longer know what you truly feel. You are in error about yourself and therefore you cannot possibly perceive and understand the other person. In many of the other so-called sins, you may be utterly aware of the original feeling. Due to certain missing links, you may be unable to feel differently, yet you know what you feel. But when you are angry, you are not feeling the primary emotion. Only with awareness can you penetrate deeper and find the underlying hurt or pain.

Many other destructive emotions, such as jealousy, envy, or lust, also contain anger. Anger may be a permanent state of the soul that is too subtle, too insidious, and too hidden even to be recognized. You will now understand the reason why I have been admonishing you to become aware of what you really feel. Whether you call it resentment or hostility, anger or hate, makes no difference; they are all the same. Most human beings are not even aware that they feel anger. Once they become aware of it, it is easier to find the underlying original emotion.

What is healthy anger? Healthy anger is objective, when justice is at stake. It makes you assert yourself. It makes you fight for what is good and true, whether the issue is your own or another's, or for a principle. You may even feel objective anger about a very personal issue, while projecting a subjective emotion upon a general issue. It is impossible to determine whether or not the emotion is healthy anger by looking only at the issue itself. Healthy anger feels very different from the unhealthy kind. Unhealthy anger poisons your system. Unhealthy anger can cause you to want to harm someone else. It calls forth your defenses and is at the same time a product of them. Healthy anger will never make you tense and guilty and ill at ease. Nor will it compel you to justify yourself. Healthy anger will never weaken you.

Any healthy feeling will give you strength and freedom, even if the outward feeling appears to be negative. An apparently positive feeling may weaken you if it is dishonest; if displacement and subterfuge are at work. If your anger leaves you freer and stronger and less confused, then it is a healthy anger. Unhealthy anger is always a displacement of an original emotion. Healthy anger is a direct emotion.

Healthy anger is like the wrath of God in the Old Testament. Righteous indignation is also healthy anger. But, you must be very careful in your self-examination. When you have an outer issue in which you may be utterly justified in feeling angry, that still may not mean that what you feel is healthy anger. The only way to determine that is by the effect your anger has on you and others. Only you can determine the truth. Only utter candor with yourself will enable you to distinguish between them.

The fifth cardinal sin is GLUTTONY. The deeper meaning of gluttony has to do with need. A need that is unfulfilled and frustrated for a long period, that is thwarted again and again, will seek unhealthy outlets. Such an outlet, among many other possibilities, may be gluttony. Why would ancient wisdom refer to this as sinful? Not merely because it is destructive of your physical health. That would certainly not be sufficient reason to call it a sin. There are many activities in a person's life which are undesirable and damaging to one's health, yet they are not considered sinful. *Something much more important and vital is at stake here.* If you are unaware of your original needs and therefore cannot go about fulfilling them through the removal of your inner obstructions, then you cannot fulfill yourself. You cannot fulfill your potential. You cannot become happy and give happiness. You cannot unfold your creative abilities. You cannot contribute, be it in ever so small a way, to human society and its development.

All human beings, no matter how much you may look down on them or may consider them insignificant, have the possibility to contribute in some way to the Soul and Earth's evolutionary plan. But only when they fulfill themselves can they do so. They cannot fulfill themselves when they are unaware of their real needs and why these needs remain unfulfilled. As they understand the reasons, thus bringing fulfillment closer and closer, they can contribute something to the vast reservoir of cosmic forces and influence evolution and their general spiritual development. The fulfillment and happiness of every human being is a necessity for the entire evolution. For as you are uplifted and fulfilled, so are the others around you, both on the planet and off the planet.

It would be unfair to say that unfulfillment is always due to selfishness. It may be selfishness, or it may be a childish self-concern. Yet there is another part of the psyche that realizes that only in happiness can one contribute, and one loses out by not contributing. This gnawing feeling of missing out makes you strive, and if you strive in the right direction, you will eventually turn inward and seek the reason for your unfulfillment. However, there are many wrong ways of striving that bring only temporary relief of the inner pressure. One of these is gluttony. There are also many other forms of addiction, such as alcoholism and drugs.

Some pastoral counselors say that masturbation is a primary addiction. How is this connected with gluttony? That this very much depends on the frequency and on the age of the person. To a degree, masturbation is normal. If it is a constant practice in adulthood, it is certainly related to gluttony, although the displacement of the real need is not quite so great. It is easier to see that the real need is a yearning for a rewarding intimate relationship on a mature basis. With gluttony, the displacement is so far removed that it is more difficult to recognize the underlying real need. However, masturbation is also a substitute. It may be an easy way out to obtain relief and release without risking the involvement and responsibility of a personal relationship.

The sixth cardinal sin is ENVY. What was said about covetousness also applies to envy. Is there something like healthy envy? No, there is not, although envy might, under certain circumstances, lead to a healthy activity. Let us say that someone is without ambition; and there is such a thing as a healthy ambition. They become lethargic, withdrawn, apathetic, and indifferent. Then this person comes into contact with someone whom he feels compelled to envy, and thus may be pulled out of his lethargic state and, perhaps, even get on the right track. A destructive feeling may have a constructive result, just as a feeling, in itself constructive, may have an unhealthy effect. It depends on the many intricacies of the human personality in relation to life circumstances. But the fact that a destructive feeling may produce positive results in certain cases does not make the feeling itself positive, healthy, or productive.

The seventh cardinal sin is SLOTH. Sloth is the indifference and apathy. Sloth represents the pseudo-solution of withdrawal from living and loving. Where there is apathy, there is rejection of life. Where there is indifference, there is laziness of the heart that cannot feel and understand others, and cannot, therefore, relate to them. Nothing produces more waste than sloth, or apathy, or withdrawal, whatever name you give it. A person who has a positive, constructive attitude toward life will not be slothful. Someone who is not preoccupied with personal safety will not withdraw, and therefore will not become apathetic. Sloth always indicates selfishness. If you are too afraid for yourself, you will not risk going forward and reaching out toward others. Whoever reaches out takes the risk of being hurt and accepts this risk as worthwhile. The benefits of sharing are greater than the feelings creating aloneness.

When you are slothful, you do not give a chance to life, to yourself, or to others. Such life-negation cannot ever be resolved unless you come to see this basic selfishness and self-concern as unhealthy. Sloth is one of the human defense mechanisms. In your fear of being hurt, you defend yourself by becoming lazy and indifferent towards everything that is life producing. Therefore sloth is rightly called a sin.

What happens with a life, from a spiritual point of view that has been wasted in sloth? The life has to be repeated, again and again, until the person finally pulls out of it. You see, a law applies here which you so often observe around you: the more you are caught in a vicious circle, the more difficult it is to break out of it. The deeper you are involved in your own conflicts and problems, which, in the last analysis, arise only because you do not want to come out of them and change, the more difficult change becomes. The more you run away from facing up to yourself and continue to resist change, the greater the difficulty becomes. This continues until your outer life becomes so unbearable that the very unhappiness finally makes you want to face it and change.

If the will to change can be mustered before life becomes so unbearable, much unhappiness can be avoided. This is why you often see that people remain caught in their inner problems as long as they somehow "get by". They seriously settle down to changing only when life is no longer bearable for them. The same holds true on a larger scale. If a life is wasted in sloth, time after time, finally the circumstances of an incarnation may become so unpleasant that the entity pulls itself together and struggles out of it.

Unfortunately, only too often sloth takes the path of least resistance as long as circumstances are not too bad. This creates for the following life the psychological condition that make it harder to live in sloth because the instinct of self-preservation finally takes over when circumstances become bad enough. When that turning point is reached depends on the person. That turning point may come in a new and more difficult incarnation, or it may occur in the course of the present life.

Hatred and fear are not mentioned. They are not considered one of the seven sins, but are also cause and effect at the same time. It is very often so in religious teachings that the effect is spoken about and not the cause. At one time, humanity was not ready to delve deeply enough to see the causes. The best that could be hoped for was to prevent people from destructive actions, even if the underlying causes were not eliminated in the individual. At least, the contagiousness and the direct outer effects of destructive actions were decreased, if not entirely eliminated. You know how contagious human behavior is. Thoughts and emotions are also contagious. In other words, outer behavior will influence outer behavior, while thought influences thought, and unconscious feelings influence unconscious feelings. The contagious actions, at least in their crassest forms, were kept in check. That is why at one time the effect was more concentrated on than the cause. Now that humanity is evolving, more attention must be given to the inner causes. We are learning how to go within *and untie the knots* through present and past life regression. Find the root cause and find the cure.

Why is fear not mentioned? Because fear is not an act, it's an involuntary emotion. It is a result of many other emotions and cannot be eliminated by a direct admonition not to fear. Fear can only be tackled by a process of psychological understanding, and by dissolving the underlying cause. If you tell people, "You must not fear because it is a sin," this will not prevent them from being frightened. They will be even more frightened. But if they slowly unroll the processes of their emotional deviations, understanding them and correcting false concepts. Then they will see that irrational fear is always selfish and separating, and they will no longer have a need for such irrational fear. It is more or less the same with hate and with anger.

The conquest of fear, as stated in the book of Matthew is by way of faith in God. How would you relate that to this teaching? Faith in God, in a genuine, secure, profound, and sincere way, can only exist if you first have faith in yourself. To the degree that you lack faith in yourself, you cannot have faith in God. Yes, you can superimpose it and deceive yourself about it, out of a need to cling to a loving authority, but it cannot be true faith unless you have gained the maturity of faith in yourself. Now, how can you have faith in yourself, unless you understand yourself as much as possible? As long as you are puzzled and grope in the dark about what effect you have on others and the effect life and others have on you, you ignore some vital information about your own psychic life. Ignorance is a result of your inner unwillingness to discover the truth, an unwillingness that is often unconscious. Overcoming the hidden resistance will make you understand yourself better and have increasing faith in yourself, and thus in God. Only in this way can you conquer fear.

The seven cardinal sins are a subtler explanation of the Ten Commandments, which are definitely based on fear, or create fear in their application. Perhaps, but every teaching, if misapplied and misunderstood, will create fear. A rigid commandment, if pronounced without the possibility of finding the underlying obstructions to following such commandments, will produce fear and guilt, and therefore hate.

Today it is no longer possible and even constructive for human beings to merely obey a commandment in their actions. Since this is not good enough, your innermost self will be fearful, even if your actions are entirely proper and conform to the commandments. The final authority is not outside of yourself, but embedded within you at your vital core. There is a vast difference between the perfectionist demands of your idealized self, and the productive life that *your real self* wants you to lead

These sins are liquid. They seem to flow into each other. Sometimes they seem like opposites, like sloth contrasted with covetousness or with gluttony. They are not exact opposites, but in some ways they are. And yet they can exist at the same time. Is there any definite connection between sloth and gluttony? The two are opposites, because gluttony is a greedy reaching out, coming from a frustrated need, while sloth is indifferent withdrawal and does not reach out. Yet both sloth and gluttony have the same common denominator: an unawareness of the original need. Both contain the cowardice that prevents people from finding that need and changing the conditions that prevent fulfillment, namely childish self-concern and selfishness. Since both sloth and gluttony come from confusion and disorder, they create more of the same.

It is perfectly true that all of these sins intermingle and overlap. They may contradict one another and yet exist simultaneously. This is so because they all have the same common denominator; since the human personality is in conflict and not one-dimensional, one level of the personality may adopt an attitude that is contradictory to another level. You can find such contradictions in yourselves and in others. This is why mature people will never think of another person as either this or that. They will perceive the contradictoriness of the human being and will be able to apply this knowledge to individual cases in their surroundings.

The sins, as well as any commandments, represent universal tendencies. The human psyche is not separated into clearly defined compartments, one compartment not having anything to do with the other, but instead one affects and influences the other. So it is with these sins. There is really no difference in weight between the seven deadly sins. Sometimes it is said that sloth is worse than pride.

Evaluating this is difficult and may be misleading. It may be true that sloth is more difficult to overcome because it is inactive. Sloth paralyzes the faculties, and thus lasts longer. But all the seven sins are symptoms of the same underlying causes.

How about sin from the spiritual point of view? If you don't actually commit the sin, though you are thinking about it, but out of fear or any other reason do not execute the sinful act, does this still count as sin?

The difference between action, feeling, or thought is not half as great as human beings want to believe. This happens especially when not committing the act is due to fear and not to love and understanding. You know that you all have an aura. What you feel and think emanates from you and is somehow always perceived by others. The higher the level of the other people's consciousness, the more aware they may be of the emanation they perceive from you. The lower their level of consciousness, the less will they be aware of it, but unconsciously they would still know. Hence your "sin" affects others, even if it is not acted out.

On the other hand, if you repress these feelings and desires out of fear and guilt, the results are even worse. You will never get to the roots and you will not understand what makes you feel that way. You will not accept yourself as you now are and will deceive yourself into believing that you are a more evolved person than you happen to be. But if you freely admit your feelings and desires, if you acknowledge them in yourself and face them, then you can find the underlying causes. Thus you will do the one thing that will free you from fear and guilt. This is how you begin to heal.

How we can heal from the temptation and desire for the seven cardinal sins.

Times are changing and uplifting our Souls, because we've moved into a new force field of energy on December 21, 2012. We are evolving and ascending simultaneously. By working with this double helix, the invisible backstage energy behind the action, anything can be healed and any knowledge can be brought forth.

Each of the Cardinal Sins hides an immensely creative human impulse, and, if we are prepared to understand their roots rather than simply indulging in self-loathing, they could help us to fulfill the very best and most life-giving potential of which we are capable.

1.)	*Envy can become an appreciation of the worth and talent of others, and a spur to develop our own gifts without resenting those of other people.*

2.)	*Gluttony can become the recognition of aspiration toward a bigger or higher reality that contributes a sense of meaning to our lives.*

3.)	*Wrath can become courage and even heroism, as well as the energy and will to take up life's hard challenges and achieve our full potential.*

4.)	*Pride can become self-respect, allowing us to express all that is most highly individual and most creative in us.*

5.)	*Lust can reveal what we find most beautiful in life, providing an experience of profound joy.*

6.)	*Deceit can become honest pragmatism and a full embrace of the reality of the world in which we must learn to move and engage.*

7.)	*Apathy can yield a profound understanding of our*

deepest emotional needs, our most cherished longings, and our grateful appreciation of the cyclical nature of life.

Your creative as well as destructive potentials of each Sin is shown by your natal chart:

Here is the Seven Deadly Sins Healing Chart. Let's begin to turn it all around to bring in Love, Peace, Harmony and even a bit of laughter.

- Envy - Finding an inner authenticity that provides deep self-esteem throughout life

- Gluttony - Discovering a powerful inner aspiration that opens new dimensions of awareness

- Wrath - Transforming rage and resentment into courage and self-affirmation

- Pride - Experiencing love of the inner Self

- Lust - Realizing a profound inner experience of beauty and joy

- Deceit - Developing the worldly wisdom that allows a grounded as well as ethical adaptation to life

- Sloth - Transmuting apathy and depression into serenity and acceptance of life's cyclical nature

May you succeed in absorbing and making this material an integral part for yourself. Much of it has not been absorbed yet. It's ahead of its time and freshly planted here to become absorbed into the human consciousness.

Only your will to plow ahead in this work of self-finding will enable you to do so. May these words fortify your understanding, both in your intellect and your emotions. Over time, these ascension vibrations will be a part of the norm as we all embrace the new language of the universe, erasing all fear and doubt to bring in the true vibrations of the higher heart: love, peace, and harmony with all beings and all things. Be blessed, each one of you, on your path, in your work, in your activities, and in your

Backstage
The Importance of Your Personal
Inner Connection

human relationships. May you all learn to accept
yourselves as you are without a feeling of sin, and in this
acceptance resolve the conditions that are called "sin".
Be in peace. Be in God!   —Mentor

CHAPTER THREE

THIS ENERGY SHIFT—ONENESS
ASCENSION—WHY NOW?

I can't love you
If I don't love me.
I can't take care of you
Until I can take care of me.
When I can love us both,
Then we can *Be*.

—Max Wiesen

What's going on with your life, here and now? If the general prognosis *is that thoughts become things*, then our highest priorities have to be our own lives. This comes along with responsibilities, challenges and opportunities. Of course we can reach out to others at anytime with caring, love, and assistance. However you cannot love others unless you love yourself. We're most helpful and at peace when we have come to peace within ourselves first. It's that simple.

This planet is in the midst of transformation and change. We claim that Mother Earth is upset with how human beings have treated her. Yes! That's true, but it reaches out further than that. Eons ago another race lived on this planet. Whether they were Atlanteians or giants doesn't matter. What does matter was the extent of their consciousness. They were well connected with the live,

25

vibrating energy that rules the Universe; a cosmic force that can fix or heal anything. They knew how to get any "prop" they needed Backstage. They went beyond human potential to a higher source of energy.

The Egyptians had healing rooms where people went in, lay down on a slab, while allowing their bodies to be worked on, using incense, flower essences, precious oils, and sound/music. The patients were encouraged to go into deep meditation to access their neuro-circuits and activate the weaker ones. It was like recharging a battery. Along with their mind power, this energy reached deep into the subconscious fields to balance and refresh any upset emotions within. When that was accomplished, the body would heal.

They could overcome pain, disease, fatigue, anger, and depression. At the same time their inner creativity, intuition and inner cosmic power would come alive and they would return to life again.

Did it work for everyone? No. Only the ones who realized and accepted that we, as humans, have the potential to tap into a higher power and heal ourselves. This takes commitment, focus, radical acceptance while embracing the all that is.

This ancient society, along with many others, knew how to activate untapped energy, empower their inner potential by merging with their eternal, true and essential self. Then something happened, the Earth changed in a flash, and these civilizations disappeared. We had to begin at the beginning.

We have come a long way throughout these thousands of years. The Earth's vibration has shifted many thousands of times. In this new millennium we stand at a pinnacle. We have reached a climax that is in process right now. We are in the "battle of our lives" and are being asked to choose between good and evil. Yes, it's not an old biblical story or children's fairy tale any longer.

Mankind has been given a rare opportunity that has been predicted and written about for these past two thousand years, or longer. We can either rise up, or perish, drowning in evil, greed, and fear. Darkness is approaching in this new decade of the 2020, and it will take every ounce of strength to walk through these next ten transformational years. It almost seems as if we're going back to the future. What will it take for you to "wake up" and understand what's really going on?

Lucky for us, the answers are here. We can be in the world, but not a part of it. We can cling to our wise inner self and depend on our inner guidance, or be swept away by the influence and desires of others. Listen up please, because there just isn't any more time.

In this world climate today, it has been difficult for many to find a continual inner peace. It's helpful to realize that it always takes two, not just one and we are all partnered off in the sense that it's us, the physical body as well as *us the Blessed Higher Self.*

The Universe works hard, on a daily basis, to bring us our desires. It's up to us to bring in the healthy energy of a higher vibration, working with our guides and angels, to manifest that which we desire. Many of us go through our lives getting up, doing our morning routine, going to work, coming home, having dinner, going to bed to get up and start all over again. The wonderment is that if you can just insert two additions to that routine, you life could change dramatically. That would be morning meditation and nightly review. "But I don't have time," you wail.

Hmmmmm! Consider this; you go to the bank, get the car gassed up or washed, buy groceries, etc., etc. Each of those activities take longer that morning meditation and nightly review. When you awaken each morning, take a deep breath and breath in the air of light. Take a moment and thank God for your coming day. Like this; "Thank you God for the beautiful breath of love and light you have given to me today. May I carry it with me throughout the day and may it touch the heart of everyone I meet. And so it is." This does wonders, believe me, and it's simple. You are giving gratitude to the Universe, and asking for blessings to others. This kind of action brings to you a slower pace, kindness, awareness, and the ability to receive wondrous new ideas to help and guide you toward whatever you need.

You and the Universe want the same things, and the Universe will completely support your thinking. These things can be summed up as health, abundance, love, peace, and harmony. This is at the center of everyone's heart, no matter who you are or where you live. Now you are taking power over your life; you are the creator, working in harmony with the Universe. Thinking—Talking—Action is your position. Unless you have been doing some negative and disarming thinking, *your dreams have to come true.* It's Natural Law.

Of course some of us look around at where and how we are living and see disharmony, disease, lack, and discomfort. So what is wrong? What can we do now? More important, how did this happen and where does the problem lie?

Elvis once sang, *"The world is a stage with each of us playing a part."* On your stage you have two people, one visible (the physical body) and one invisible, (the Blessed Higher Self or the real You). Anyone and everyone else is a participant in your life and they are there for one of three reasons; to love and support you, to parent and teach you, or to cause a disturbance. No matter what, they are helping with the growth of your Soul. The most awesome truth in this fact is that you called them all, yes all, in to help you move closer to your spiritual Soul.

Then we have nightly review, which is of utmost importance. As your day draws to a close, and you prepare to sleep, keep a journal by your bedside. Think about your day and how it unfolded for you. Write down something you have gratitude for. It doesn't have to be much, but something important to you. Perhaps your grandson took his first step, perhaps your son or daughter called you from a distance, perhaps an unexpected check arrived in the mail. Anything that can make you smile and feel warmhearted. Then give thanks for that happening.

That's part one of nightly review. Next, think about whether something made you feel uncomfortable or out of sorts. Perhaps you had a disagreement or words with someone.

Ask yourself two questions.
1) How did I bring this to myself? And
2) How can I love it?

Then know that you have twenty-four hours to make amends. Within that time do the best you can to bring the incident up to a higher level.

If you do have a disagreement, meditate on why this happened. What was going on inside of you, how were you off kilter? Louise Hay always said, "You're never angry at what you think you're angry at. Mostly, you're angry with yourself." Find forgiveness in your heart for the incident and mostly for yourself.

This is how you get out of the jungle, the tangled, confusing life you're living, I know you may find this a bit difficult to accept, and it may seem too easy. Well, indeed it is. It's simple and a personal and private thing. However, through developing this type of consciousness, you are healing the mind, body, and soul. Nothing will bother you or keep you awake nights because you have it handled. Take the time.

Make this a universal spiritual practice and watch as the basis and vibration of the world shifts. This is one way your Master Soul can heal and use its Soul Power to influence and transform all life.

Heal and allow the transition of your Soul first—then the transformation and healing of all of life will follow.
— Mentor.

Backstage
The Importance of Your Personal
Inner Connection

NOTES:

CHAPTER FOUR
THE OVERSHADOW AND HOW IT WORKS

Open my eyes to the world –
the world that shines in you.
Open my heart to the world
the world that beats with you.
For my life that's shining free –
I give all I am to Thee
Oh open my eyest to the world.
— *William Vitalis*

Many of us are seeking to be in alignment with the flow of
energy spiraling down to Earth from the center of our
Galaxy. These Universal energies contain all knowledge of
all the Universes combined as ONE, and are available to
everyone who can reach up and access them, through use of
the *New Spiritual Chakras*. When you develop yourself
through these exercises, you are *overshadowed* by an
invisible energy force; as long as you keep working with
your inner self and these mind exercises, something
happens that is yet unexplained but true. You are
"protected". You intuitive abilities are strengthened, and
you sense less and less anxiety and fear. This fact, of

course, helps your inner body perform well and keeps you centered and clear headed.

All of us need to strengthen our invisible force field. It's time to re-establish your mind and body with the energies of your Soul. Once you have established this connection within, through focused meditation, it will strengthen you as well as help to guide you as you walk your path. The petals of your Soul are opening, along with the NEW Spiritual Chakras, and a brilliant amber Light is pouring into the center of your being, into your aura, body and heart.

Sometimes we don't really realize what our inner being is, our unconscious, and all that it holds. As we go through life, we have our ups and downs, our loving days as well as our sad days. We can bury things, desires, or memories of past events. We figure that we cannot do much to change it, and all of a sudden, that which we have held within us and thought about for years and years comes up again and manifests. It seems like a coincidence and you ask yourself, "How did Spirit know?" How did the Universe know that this is what I've been thinking about or secretly desired? Of course Spirit knows, because it's held in the part of your being that you cannot see. It's tucked away in your heart. *Spirit always knows your thoughts, prayers, and desires before you even ask.*

The Universe answers the desire in its own time and its own way through a vibration of Light. If you feel like you've been in the wrong job, or you don't have the right career or perhaps the right partner, or you're discouraged about what's going on around you, SIT and take the time to reconnect and establish your Soul-mind connection. Ask for purity, clarity, and face the Light. Face the Love and warmth as it beams in to you. It can be difficult for some people because they do not understand how this energy works.

For anything to manifest, it must happen on all levels. By that I mean that if you're ready for a new job or new relationship, Spirit begins to "clear the pathway" for that manifestation immediately. However, what we don't usually think about is that the object, place, or person coming into our lives must be ready for the change as well. This is true so that all can be in balance because the *Natural Laws of the Universe* are always clear and balanced.

People have allowed themselves to become a recluse, being alone, or not being listened to; that's why the computer and electronic devices are so popular and prevalent. When you are being abused you forget what its like to have the cosmic Light and love come in. When the Light does reach them, they doubt it or try to find a motive, or find an excuse to defile and change the purity of the Light. They make assumptions that muddy the pond so the White Lotus blossom rising up through the mud gets splattered on, decreasing the power of the Light beam and perhaps snuffing it out by not accepting it.

Try to realize that the Cosmic Light is your breath, the Cosmic Light is the breeze that flows across a field. This Light flows naturally around and through your physical body and encircles your entire being. It even can clear your Aura if you can get yourself into a meditative state and raise your vibration. There are many simple and wonderful ways to do this. This Light is the caretaker, nurturer, and affectionate devotee to your Garden of Light. You're the creator, you have *planted the seeds to grow* with your life decisions.

Whatever you have experienced in life is because of your stream of thought and decisions. Take a look at your thoughts and decisions over the past six months or so, then see what you can do to bring them to a healthier, higher, living space. This is why people get discouraged. They feel like everything they want doesn't come. But instead of truly believing that it all can manifest, they throw in blocks and doubts.

It will never happen.
I'm not deserving.
Maybe it will happen or maybe it won't.
I'm tired of waiting.
I give up!

When you think that way what happens is the vibrational current of energy gets confused. It doesn't know whether to come towards you or to dissipate, and you

33

create something called a block. A block is just as sacred as what your wish is and has to be honored in the same manner. It honors you while you can't seem to make up your mind. Therefore you create a *block that stuns you* and you are not able to move forward.

Remember, the energy, the Cosmic Flow, Holy Ghost, or mind/body flow, whatever you want to call it, is here to support you and help you overcome the blocks of your desires. It helps you to comprehend the TRUTH of the Creator, which is always to please you, always to bring you Love and support. The energy is on the Earth to lift you up, to give you strength, to bring you up to the highest level of vibration that you can endure; also to bring in that which you are talented with and what you desire. It is your mother, your father, your sister, and your brother — The supporting family of Light around your Soul.

Your Soul is your Soul, or God-center. You became a person that manifested on Earth through a decision with your Soul. The Soul shines through all of the *Inner Planes* of your Body/Mind/Spirit and sometimes we don't know where these planes are or how deep they are. Every word you utter, every thought you have, every experience you live through creates an imprint on your Soul. When Bette Midler sang. *"God is watching you, From A Distance,"* I wondered if she realized how true that beautiful song is.

The time has come for us to take the time to develop the unity of our Soul with our Earth bodies to establish a line of connection. In that way, we'll be able to receive constant guidance through this next decade as well as through troubled times.

The summer of 2019 brought us some shocking energy and surprises. We are learning as a race, some great lessons. The future is changing along with our personal thoughts. We are in the process of leaving behind whatever it is that we don't want to take into our future. Your closure timeline can be activated whenever your ready. As 2020 opens prepare to end your personal cycle, make sacrifices necessary for your integrity, tap in and use the potential energy that is always there for you. Significant decisions must be made before 2020 comes to a close.

Justice can be served in a peaceful fashion. We are at just the beginning of this new decade. This is when the true colors come out about some high ranking people and others. Everyone scrambles to stop it, but it cannot be stopped. Buried matters will be re-triggered, and this energy will be released as others look for the truth. Our world and thoughts will be shaken in ways that will be shocking and upsetting.

Some people will be cornered while others will be exonerated. The scales are being reset during this new century. People who are out of integrity, lying, stealing, cheating, and living only for self will not be able to get away with it anymore. A veil is placed over those who move forward with ill intentions toward others.

If you chose to balk with this new direction, you will be stuck with that stubborn, heavy and dark energy for the next twelve years. This new energy will meet your standards. It can trap you or free you. It's all your choice.

People will not tolerate being kept in the dark or thrown away any longer. When you embrace the love that is flowing on the Earth, you will be supported. For order, natural law, courage, fairness, and integrity meet victory. Abandon all and walk the walk, even though you may feel that a compromise has to be made.

In the dark, snowy, cold, winter months, when Pluto turned direct, conjunct Saturn and Jupiter in mid-January, 2020, a massive upheaval came, catching everyone off guard. This awareness may bring the time when you will clearly see if you are stuck or on your new timeline.

The key here is receiving messages, not through channeling or "someone from the other side", but reach higher into the depths of the Double Helix energy, to actually align and be in tune with the *messages or whispers of your Soul* through the grace of Spirit. You will go beyond the Astral Plane into the eternity of the Universe. There you will connect with the *Golden Thread of Wisdom*. (Grammie Hemphill- from *Unlimited Realities*)

This alignment explores the depths and foundation of your life and all past lives. It enables you to experience the inexhaustible wellspring of information and realize how the Divine can be interwoven within your nature.

Backstage
The Importance of Your Personal
Inner Connection

Ask yourself this while looking into a mirror: What is important and significant now? What is left behind the rubble of the winds of change?

Try this mantra: *"I am going to love myself, holding myself responsible for my actions, not allowing abuse of any sort to touch my life, and walk my road to manifest my new beginning. People from my past may try to come back. However, I will never return to the 'old ways.' With great love, kindness, and support from the Universe, I will move along my new timeline, putting out and receiving love and abundance."*

From now on and throughout your life your will focus upon the mechanism of self-change, and begin to integrate unconscious motive with conscious intent. As my teacher, Louis Hay, always taught, you must first draw from the well of the Divine to nourish and give to your *self*. Then there will be more than enough to give to others. You will begin to feel a sense of "family solidarity" with every breath, every feeling, and every word or action.

We're moving into a time in humanity's present and future (through this decade and the next two) when souls will have less of a chance to incarnate again because of personal actions and intentions *against* life – human beings' freewill choosing *against* the Light.

The vibrations of the times are ever moving higher, and the times will not have for humans an avenue to be born within arenas/circumstances of the lower vibrations, which in turn, would facilitate humans in continuing to manifest lower vibration (hate-centered) actions. This is a natural process because of the spiritual principle of "Like attracts like". In other words, in most dimensions, we gravitate to the vibration level at which we personally vibrate.

There will be other processes, arenas and circumstances, with other physical/Earth-like environments, whereby any of us will be able to face ourselves, and our own karma. Many of us will be on the Earth of the future. Even with this vibration induced limitation, no soul shall be forgotten or metaphorically "left behind" or left without a path which will help those souls to find the Light.

To help understand this further, as this process of raising the vibrations builds in the Earth, which comes from the efforts of billions of souls, there will be fewer and fewer opportunities for those souls who seek to manifest dark (non-love centered) activities to enter during these times of higher vibration. The strength of this effort means that there will be fewer souls able to incarnate into their higher vibratory level, which would otherwise allow many Souls opportunities to decide to turn their path towards the Light.

Those described here will be denied Earth opportunities for many years and some for thousands of years and a few for eons, because the vibratory level will not be available. These Souls will be in limbo for these years, with little opportunity to work out karmic debts – except within one's self. Only one's self and one's actions is conscious until the strength of the higher levels is available. The darkness will be diminished from vastly fewer souls on the Earth plane and from the internal shadows within human souls coming forth within human consciousness because of the unwillingness to resolve any of our internal shadows previously.

While some may see this as a punishment, or even unfair, it is not. This process is one where we are hindered from making things worse for ourselves. In other words, our own behavior and thought patterns are such that we would only make things worse for ourselves if allowed to incarnate back into the Earth at times of darkness or lower vibrations.

Sometimes a soul doesn't care if they make things worse for oneself. One's only thought is how can we cause pain and suffering onto others, because the pain and suffering within ourselves is so great and we want others to know our pain.

We have the healing key within each of us to heal the pain and suffering. The key is this: *The experiences we create for others are the same experiences we create for ourselves.* The pain and suffering – or the peace and healing experiences we create for others to go through are the same experiences we will go through. Everyone is part of the *Infinite Consciousness of God*. We create experiences as part of the Infinite Consciousness and of which all of the Infinite Consciousness experiences, including our Self/Soul as part of that Infinite Consciousness.

This is one of many motivating factors for billions of souls currently on the Earth (and off the Earth) to choose healing paths for our selves and others. The healing we choose for others is the healing we choose for ourselves. Likewise, the pain we choose to inflict on others is the pain we are choosing to inflict on ourselves. Healing examples of this can be seen in the actions of those who seek to and are motivated to help others, regardless of the arena this help may be directed to. In essence, they are answering the call to heal themselves (albeit unconsciously), as well as other lifetimes.

An allegory for this time period can be read in the Revelations book of the Bible. 1000 years of peace is our destiny, but only when we build the foundation for it to begin. Then after this time, the book says *"the devil will be let loose again"*.

Yes, this is related to the time Christ returns, but only God knows when that will be. However, we can build a foundation for it via our inner work, our prayers, our meditations and healing of our relationships. As we raise the vibrations of the planet, we are creating relationships and an environment whereby the Christ Spirit becomes welcome. In essence, this process and work refers to the phrase and message of *"I stand at the door and knock"*. Our inner work, and the subsequent manifestation of that inner work in the relationships and environments in which we live our lives, show whether or not we open the door for a great Love to enter into our Earth. "I stand at the door and knock" is not just referring to our own hearts, minds and souls, but also the Earth itself.

The saving grace for all souls is "We have eternity to work this out within ourselves." and "No soul shall be abandoned." The vibrating energy never stops and is always uplifted from the other, higher, swirling energies.

"We cannot move beyond karma, when our hands are holding the karmic chains we place on ourselves and others." —Mentor

Backstage
The Importance of Your Personal
Inner Connection

NOTES:

CHAPTER FIVE
WHERE HAVE YOU BEEN PLACED?
HURRY UP!

Things are happening so faaaasssst! Things are happening
in the world, in our country, in our area, and in my own life
with such rapidity that it's difficult to absorb it, assimilate
it or comprehend it. It's good to know that we all are in the
midst of some sort of transformation. No one knows how
this is going to pan out, especially for those who don't want
it. It certainly seems totally confusing. Many have been
feeling light headed, dizzy, and out of sorts since the spring
of 2019. The energy on the planet has been so strong and so
new that many don't know how to deal with it.

     I have always sought Truth and have been blessed,
perhaps more so than others, with parents, grandparents,
friends, teachers and experiences that have helped me
along the path; especially during the year of 2019. It is
astonishing to me that I could feel so confused.

     Some decades ago, I realized that in the Springtime,
there is a release. A *spiritual potency* seems to arrive every
March at the Spring Equinox such as no other time of the
year. Each year in the Spring, I have received, without fail,
some new spiritual awareness. However, this past year the
power of the new energy was that of any ten springs
combined.

     The spring of 2019 was power packed with a
stronger energy stream from both the Sun and the center of

the galaxy. Just before my birthday on March 16th, I received a call from Donna, a long-standing client who lives in Austin, Texas. I had been to Texas several times and liked Austin a lot. I've always said I would never live in Texas, but if I had to it would only be in Austin.

For several years my prayer had been to be released from the relationship I was existing in. It had become very toxic as well as dangerous for me. As you may well know, a person cannot "see" their karma for themselves. No matter how "psychic" they are. Monika, a close friend of mine who has excellent intuition skills, had a dream about me a year or so prior. She told me I would have the opportunity to leave my husband. She warned me that it would only be given to me once, and my choice would be very important. She asked me to go within and find my strength. She advised me to trust and told me I would be fine. It was time for me to know myself and trust myself.

As we approached the Spring Equinox, Don and I reached a point of no return. On some level, I feared for my life everyday. Part of me did not realize that I constantly carried this fear within. It was too old and familiar because I had the fear from past lives, and in this life as soon as I took my first breath.

From our combined Astrological Charts, I knew Don and I had shared many a past life. I was also aware that I was working through the karma with my father. When my identical twin sister became ill in late 2012, I began working with two of the best energy healers in the world; Luisa Rasiej (Italy) and Pujhita (Japan). At that time Luisa lived near me in Bucks County, PA.

Six years had passed since my sister, foster daughter and best friend had died, all within six months of each other. Much of my support system had left, and I needed to focus and continue to untie the knots of karma that kept me so tightly bound. Spiritually, through my meditations, I sensed that the Lightworkers had to be "placed" by 2020. We are being readied for the coming battle of darkness. The Divine and higher beings were preparing all of us to "hold the Light," as the people of the planet began their battle with each other. This would last through 2027 but not be complete until 2038. I knew I could not stay in my situation. I just would not make it.

Donna was calling to see if I planned to come out to Austin soon. I said I'd come as soon as some work arrived. She asked me to come visit and offered to get a few friends together for a class and meditation weekend. Feeling a soft wind of fresh air flow through me, I gladly agreed. We planned the visit for Holy week, just before Easter.

By the time I arrived in Austin, I had decided to make a move. Donna felt Austin would be a good place for my work, so she arranged for me to work with a realtor to look for housing. I rented the third house shown to me that day, and returned to Bucks County with a new address, PO Box and phone number. Talk about fast. Within two weeks I relocated to North Austin Texas from a twenty-year marriage and home. It felt like pulling of a Band-Aid quickly. There was no time to think, just pack and move. With thought and planning, I was out of that house in one day.

Joy flowed through me during the five-day drive out to Austin. I enjoyed visiting some friends along the way, and looked forward to my new adventure. On the way, I received an email from Pujhita asking me if I would be doing the annual tour with Amma in June. She wanted me to help with her Radiance Healing table. My heart soared as I agreed.

I had six weeks to "settle in," unpack, and learn more about my surroundings. My days were full with unpacking, furniture shopping, organizing my office, the kitchen, personal items, etc. Before I knew it, June 20th had arrived and I was off to Santa Fe, New Mexico to begin the 2019 Summer tour with Amma. Working at the Radiance Healing table with Pujhita and many friends was heartwarming and healing for me. We went to Santa Fe, Dallas, Atlanta, New York, and Marlborough, Mass.

My friend, Marie Ann came to Amma's program in Marlborough from Manchester, NH, and asked me to stay with her so some of us could go to the beach at Kennebunkport, ME, for a few days of rest. Amma's tour finished on a Thursday, and Marie Ann and I drove up to Manchester, New Hampshire; about a two-hour drive. We planned to drive to Maine on Monday, so the weekend was clear.

My mother was born in New Hampshire and I have several relatives living in that area. I had spent every summer at "Grammies house" in Warner, my mother's place of birth. On Saturday afternoon I asked Marie Ann if she wanted to go up to Warner so I could visit my parents, grandparents, and cousin Kathy's graves. Kathy had passed away that last October, and we were as close as sisters.

We stopped in Concord to pick up some flowers and plants, and drove the nineteen miles up through the Mink Hills to Warner, a small town that sits at the base of Mt. Kearsarge. I have loved that ride ever since I was a small child. Whenever I meditate and ask for centering and peace, I close my eyes and picture this drive and the glory of the Mink Hills.

As we arrive at the cemetery a dim, lighted mist descended from the heavens. I went over to Kathy and my parents graves first, stood still a minute, and "felt" a vibration coming from each grave. Marie Ann felt it as well and we both agreed it was like a heartbeat. I walked over to my grandparents' and uncle's graves, and felt the same vibration. It was beginning to shake me up a bit. I knew it was some kind of message from the other side and understood that my relatives were trying to tell me something.

Looking over at Marie Ann, I said, "Let's go up to the house. I wasn't going to ask you to, but there's some kind of a message here, and I feel it's important to take a ride by." She agreed. We lingered a few minutes longer, and then were on our way.

From the time I was very small, my Grandmother had told me I would be spending my last days at her house, during the "Last Days". However, the house was taken from the family after my father died and I had purged it from my system in 1984. The house was sold in 1991, and strangers had been living there all these years. They had changed the color and several other things. It just wasn't the same anymore.

My Grandfather had built that house and completed it in 1910. My mother and her siblings had grown up there. It was definitely the Hemphill Homestead and the land, although not level, was spectacular. The property has a brook running behind it as well as a natural spring.

Grammie was the daughter of Jenny Patch, who was from Maine and part Penobscot, a section of the Algonquin Tribe. She had trained her daughter to know the land and everything in it. Grammie was a true Shaman as well as a "far seer" as she was lovingly called.

Marie Ann and I got back to the car, and drove up Kearsarge Street to Kirkland, turned left, then drove over to Roslyn Ave. This is known as the back way to the house. As we turned left again and approached the house, Marie Ann let out a shout, "Elizabeth, the house is empty and it's for sale." She parked the car in front, by the mailbox and for sale sign. Then we just turned and silently stared at each other.

Shortly we both got out and Marie Ann went around looking in the windows, while I took a picture of the for sale sign with my Iphone.

"What are you going to do?" Marie Ann asked.

"I'm not sure, but I'm calling the realtor to find out more." I responded, shaking. I wanted to find out the price and see the inside of the beloved house. I was feeling completely overwhelmed. After all, I had just run away from Bucks County, PA to Austin, Texas to save my life. Now, here I am in Warner, New Hampshire, and Grammies house is for sale.

I'm an astrologer and I was aware of the rare astral energies that were going on at this time. Globally, we're in a battle of the old versus the new. The idea being, "Don't hang on to the old. Release it and move forward into your new life." Talk about confusion!

Saturday night I did a lot of thinking and meditation, while talking the matter over with a close friend. I called the Realtor and made an appointment for the next afternoon. To make matters worse, Mercury was retrograde. My inner thoughts were, "Why is this happening now, and is it going to work out?" Well, I should have known better.

Backstage
The Importance of Your Personal
Inner Connection

Marie Ann and I drove back to Warner Sunday afternoon on July 13th, 2019. It was my father's birthday. Somehow I sensed that Amma was behind all this. If anyone could see, feel, and manipulate the deep, subconscious energies, She was the one to do so.

Rhonda, the realtor, was very knowledgeable and filled me in on the history of the house since it had passed out of the family. The kitchen had been remodeled, the bathroom updated, and some cosmic things done. However, there still was some very expensive work that needed doing. The price being asked was high, so we began negotiating. I found myself purchasing the house for the price I was willing to pay, which was $20,000 less than the asking price. I did buy the house, of course.

CHAPTER SIX
ALIGNING WITH HIGHER LEVELS OF LIGHT

You are the one,
Every moment is your opportunity,
and now is the time.

EAJ (8/9/2019)

We live in an incredible time, one in which there continues to be new waves of light streaming onto the planet. Gateways opening, DNA activating, hearts opening, and more and more people "waking up" to the reality of the powerful period of ascension. We're living through a gateway, an opening, with new levels of light streaming onto the planet day by day.

It's a time when the changes unfolding now in your personal life, the dramas playing out on the world stage, and the shifts and changes happening on a personal, planetary, and collective scale have an underlying higher purpose. In the wise words of Paramahansa Yogananda *"A Divine universal plan exists and it is beautiful and full of joy."*

And here's the thing, the Full Moon Eclipse in Cancer on December 25, 2019, was a marker in time that signifies a light gateway opening. Triggering a wave of light, frequency, and awakening to elevate the vibration of Humanity and Earth, which is such a beautiful thing, can

47

also tend to stir things up. Over the next few months, and throughout the year of 2020, our *Transition* year, remember that we're in the period of calm before the storm.

Keep cleaning and clearing out what no longer serves and supports your highest self. Create some space to meditate and visualize for what you want to see manifest spiritually and in your physical life. In other words, if you haven't worn it, donate it! If it doesn't uplift you, sell it. Let it go! Let it all go.

Take the time to meditate, recharge, vibe up, and align your mind and entire being with the vibrational frequency of what you really want to see in your life as well as on a global scale. This wave of light energy will reach its peak during the Solar Eclipse on the Summer Solstice, June 20, 2020. With conscious intention, you're able to use this time band to align with the higher vibrational timeline of light. Yes! A higher vibrational experience is available to you, but you have to choose it; you have to consciously and vibrationally align with.

Exactly what will this look like for you? Honestly, this is in part up to you to decide. What are you open for and willing to receive? What are you becoming a vibrational match with? True abundance? Radiant Love? Peace, light, and bliss for all beings? To have a greater alignment with your authentic truth and highest light? Every moment within this time period is your opportunity to choose wisely: To choose love, and to vibrationally lift your soul up to a higher level of living.

Now, if you slip into lower energies—Reset! If you stumble—get back up! Remember that we're all in this together and you now have access to so much incredible invisible support that is available. Keep asking your guides and angels for help and continue looking inward.

Clearing The Lower Levels to Ascend

To fully ascend into total enlightenment and awareness of the Divine within yourself and within everything— everywhere, you need to being by clearing out the old and outdated patterns, habits, beliefs and judgmental energies. This is paramount to make room for the inner brilliance and illumination of Divine light to shine through you.

By cutting the cords to the past, and releasing the pain, guilt, or grief, which is weighing you down, you free yourself to awaken and begin to ascend. You're then able to shine as the unique expression of the Divine Love that you are, moving forward on your path of illumination.

Ascension caught quite a buzz leading up to and around 2012. but now that that date has long come and gone. With the arrival of the Double Helix energies, which have been active since that date, it's more clear now than ever before, that instead of something external magically helping all to shift at once, *it's now up to you all* by individually going inward.

It's up to each and every individual to make the inner shift to awaken and ascend. Then, collectively we are able to view reality through the lens of love, and through this new, enlightened perspective. The 'mass ascension' and the realm of love on Earth can be fully felt and seen. It's universally very powerful.

Thanks to continued waves of light and spiritual energy flowing onto Earth from the center of our galaxy and the Divine realms, Ascension is now more than ever before, available to all. More people are waking up everyday to the feeling and knowing that there is more to life than money, the economy, and the physical aspects of reality. Through *one person at a time*, a wave of awareness is growing around the world. The once hidden teachings of love, enlightenment, and ascension are no longer concealed by mystery schools, religions, and secret societies. The books, teachings, and information have been made available to everyone, and will continue to be uncovered as we grow.

The information is out there, and the stage is set. However, Ascension takes commitment, and self responsibility to make the permanent leap out of fear, and into Love. It takes a constant return to awareness to shift out of old patterns and habits in order to 'lift into the light', to evolve, and Ascend. This is why morning meditation and nightly review is so very important. It's called *Tying into the energies*.

How Do You Ascend?

To Ascend is to infuse your consciousness with the infinite possibilities and unlimited realities that manifest through love and acceptance. The Ascension path is multidimensional, and involves all that you are on every level. Lifting your Self up to experience new levels of Divine Light is one aspect of the ascension path. Releasing, integrating and healing past wounds, energetic blockages, beliefs, fears, and limitations is another. When you do both there is a greater success and this happens quickly. It's known as untethering.

Throughout the Ascension process, awareness is essential.

With awareness you are able to know your required work and your next steps. You're able to notice the patterns and beliefs holding you in density and release them in the moment to step into a new level of love. The ascension path is not easy, but it is simple. You simply have to be willing to radically surrender and let go. Your awareness is your most valuable resource, and so if you want to progress on your ascension path, make a commitment to take control of your emotions and become more and more aware. In the physical world now there is a constant supply of distractions entertaining and stimulating our minds in every moment. Detach, Unplug. The mind is part of what we are training to release; whatever is unnecessary. But to do so we need to be able to allow it to pause.

Turn off the TV, put down the smart phone, and just be and breathe. Learn to meditate and *pause your mind on demand* for this increases your awareness, and with awareness you're able to consciously interact with the world around you; to learn and validate truth through real life experience.

It's also important to prepare your body vehicle for higher levels of Light through detoxification and clearing lower levels of emotions, limiting beliefs and fear.

Awareness will also help you to adapt to the ever-changing circumstances of life around you.

In addition to meditation, learn and seek out new perspectives, validate what you learn to gain wisdom and knowledge, then implement what will serve you. Love every moment of this expanding consciousness phase, continue to move forward, and grow. This is the Ascension Path of Light; the path of increased awareness, higher consciousness, and illumination. The Master Path of Love.

Higher vibrational living awaits you as you consciously choose to ascend. It is more than worth it to put in the time to meditate, to open your heart, link with the Divine and with the realms of spirit as well as to release that which is not in alignment with who you are becoming. Your awareness is key. Pay attention to what gets your attention. What makes your heart move? Is it love? Is what you are filling your mind and body with serving you in your life and on your ascension path? It is fueling your soul and spirit or just distracting you?

Not all will ascend in this lifetime. But if you were drawn to read this book, the stage is set for you! Your total enlightened and illuminated self already exists and is cleared and active. Now it's simply a matter of integrating your Amber Light and new heart center into your being by bringing your spiritual power into the physical body. Opening your heart, becoming aware, and shining with the full brilliance of your higher self and spiritual being can be here in the physical.

Inserting the Divine Healing Seals into the Chakras
Denotes using Chakras 0 through 12

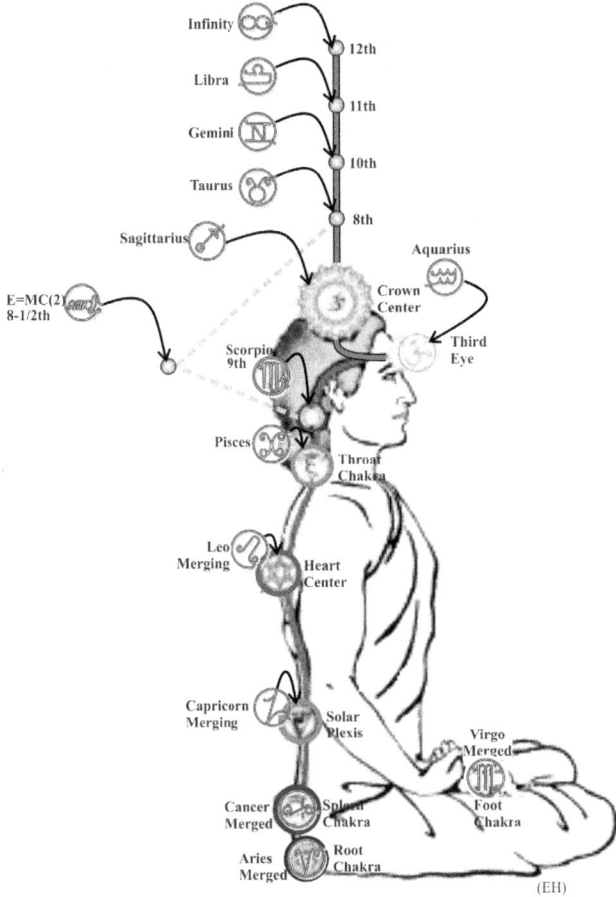

Infinity

12th

Libra

11th

Gemini

10th

Taurus

8th

Sagittarius

Aquarius

E=MC(2)
8-1/2th

Crown
Center

Scorpio
9th

Third
Eye

Pisces

Throat
Chakra

Leo
Merging

Heart
Center

Capricorn
Merging

Solar
Plexis

Virgo
Merged

Cancer
Merged

Spleen
Chakra

Foot
Chakra

Aries
Merged

Root
Chakra

(EH)

The NEW Spiritual Chakras

OPENING THE TWELVE CHAKRAS
A SIDE VIEW

Elizabeth Joyce

CHAPTER SEVEN

**FLOWING WITH AND ACCEPTING
THE NEW WORLD**

With the winds that shall come, to change that which needs changing, understand and know and trust that every one of those light particles that you part with will go forth transforming other's lives; along with that know that not now or not ever will you be alone.

The Earth is now knee-deep in economic meltdown. Every day you have reminders of the ailing financial systems of key countries such as the United States. On a personal level, you likely have your own reminders of the fragile nature of the economic infrastructure of your now global society. You have learned to depend upon these financial systems, and to expect that they would always be there in the familiar forms.

To be sure, it's a big wake up call to discover that what you had thought reliable and strong is indeed crumbling beneath your feet. There is a natural feeling of loss associated with this, regardless of how you are personally impacted right now. This feeling of loss can be overwhelming, and it can trigger a sudden episode of depression. Even if you don't typically become depressed, you can feel like a black cloud is obscuring your happiness, hopes and dreams.

53

Backstage
The Importance of Your Personal
Inner Connection

The Tipping Point

While comparisons are being made between this current crisis and America's great depression of the 1930's, today's economic predicament is quite different. The world has reached a tipping point, and the out-of-balance structures will need to be addressed in order for humanity to move forward. Band-aids will not suffice. The global distress cannot be resolved through local measures that are isolationist, protectionist, or elitist.

What you are witnessing and experiencing is part of the great reconfiguration underway as humanity births a new paradigm world. Finances are coming under the spotlight first, as this sector is closely interconnected with society's other outmoded structures.

It's really not personal, this crisis, yet it certainly can feel quite personal when your income, your bank account, and even your sense of long term financial security appear to be uncertain. Separate from this, of course, you may well have suffered economic losses on a number of fronts since 2008.

In addition, you may be dealing with a variety of other types of loss, some already manifest and some possible in your near future. This is like a magnification factor, potentially heightening conscious and subconscious fears of the unknown. You may even feel anxiety when simply contemplating the prospect of how much really needs to change on the planet. A wise part of you knows that change and loss are normal elements of the creation process on Earth. You likely have witnessed or directly experienced countless losses - big and small—throughout your life. Most likely, you have developed coping mechanisms for handling loss. Some of these you may be aware of, and others may be unconscious.

Your wise self (higher self) also knows that the changes happening now on the planet are a part of the great shift in consciousness you have come to witness and birth. Remember, we all chose to be here at this time of human evolution. The road now is indeed rocky, yet where it leads is a place in which you, as a being, can soar with the Wind

Right now, given the prospect of *the window of time you are passing through,* is an excellent moment to contemplate and perhaps update and upgrade your responses to change and loss. As a reminder, this unique window of time involves an opportunity for you to catapult yourself into great lightness of being. Your ability to shift out of past limiting patterns and to remember the truth of who you are is profound beyond measure in this lifetime; especially in this particular cycle. The acceleration and magnitude of what is before you cannot be quantified in human terms. *Never before has there been so much cosmic assistance* or such a collective global shifting in consciousness as you will witness now, during the next six to nine months, and during this window of time. Therefore, taking a close look at your relationship with change will be well worth the effort it takes.

If you lived at the seashore and it was hurricane season, you would naturally want to take precautions to protect your home and family. You and your neighbors, certainly, would consider boarding up the house and packing the family car with provisions as needed. Similarly, right now with the massive reconfiguration happening in plain view, you and your human companions are being nudged to discover more evolved responses to change, instead of shivering with fear in the dark.

The typical human being has become like a fat man wearing a suit three sizes too small and trying to fit his oversize body on standard size chairs designed for people of his grandparents' generation. His overweight body is causing a growing list of health problems as well.

This man, in order to be comfortable and healthy, has a number of options, each one of them involving some sort of change. The key for this man is HOW he approaches this necessary change. That challenge has everything to do with consciousness, and where, energetically, the man sits in each moment as he responds to the happenstance of his personal life along with the events happening in his world.

The energy of how the man sits is the key. The man can choose what sort of cushion he sits on, impacting how he sees and experiences his world. However, this ordinary man either tends to forget he has this choice, or perhaps he simply has not learned that he has a choice. After all, this

55

vital training is nonexistent in most cultures who are focused on outer world success.

Choose Your Chair and Your Cushion

If you sit on a cushion of separation, fear and hate, you will face great obstacles during these times of massive change. The old paradigm ways involving fear and blame will not get you where you want to go. Judging yourself and others for how things are will keep you in the negative spiral of energy that you are looking to escape from.

Expecting others to rescue you, or to magically fix your problems, will leave you feeling even more disempowered. Viewing the disassembly of your broken systems as disaster — will add to your sense of loss and hopelessness. Each person, in order to thrive in the coming months and years, will need to learn more innovative and light-filled ways to respond to what's happening, including learning a new language.

Going Deeper

For you personally, that means getting to know yourself more intimately. If you think you already know yourself, remember that the path of self-awareness is an ongoing learning process. To succeed at the more advanced levels, one must be willing to go deeper and to look at oneself in new ways. This sometimes means revisiting topics that seem like a rehash of old news.

Therefore, consider right now—opening yourself to some radically new options and ideas. Check in with your Heart Chakra and begin the flow of a more positive energy that will begin shifting your experience of what's happening to your world now.

What To Do:

1. Decide today that you will learn a fresh approach to working with change and loss.

2. Ask your Blessed Higher Self to help you become more comfortable with the process of change, and to stay more positive when you lose jobs, possessions, and people dear to you.

3. Invite in the help of Spirit to lovingly show you new productive responses to change.

4. Imagine or visualize regularly throughout your day, starting now, that you are surrounded and supported by a host of benevolent physical and nonphysical helpers.

Remember that the changes needed on our planet and within the Solar System will come from people like yourself who begin to make different choices and learn to find their center amidst the chaos. A part of you, now existing in the future, has already done this. Call upon this part of yourself now, and regularly, as you travel the uncertain road ahead. As you continue the journey of rediscovering your Divine nature, know you are surround with love and blessings.

The Earth is accelerating in vibration as we move through this new decade. We can assist the Earth in this acceleration process by becoming the bridges to a higher vibrating star energy available through this solar system.

In Oneness — The Mind Harmonizes With The Heart

During this past decade, there has been a huge focus on re-orienting you to your Lower Heart Chakra. This was necessary for balance in the progressive movement toward wholeness. So many of you have, for years, lived primarily within your minds; re-orienting you to the heart is critical to facilitating a sense of Unity and the desire to BE-love. Now, we have emerged into a domain of wholeness and Oneness. Within Oneness, we re-claim the vital and beautiful aspect of the mind, incorporating and aligning it in harmonious balance with the heart, and joining that to the higher heart center — the Tenth Chakra!

Mental focus is a requirement for clarity and function. It is not possible to have a productive and happy human life without learning to make peace with your mind. Your mind, and your thinking capabilities give form to your energy! They send out mind signals that organize and synthesize your experience; similar to the signal vibrations that cause your inner organs to move and work in perfect time. The awareness you experience exists in part through your minds ability to discern what information to share and make present to you. As you cultivate your relationship to your mind, your mind, like a cable box on the TV, learns what "programs" you prefer and starts to orient around your preferences! This is the wonderful, adaptive and amazing power of your mental faculty and your mind!

Thinking is an important and highly creative aspect of the human experience. Now that you have reconnected with an orientation to oneness and unity, and have opened your hearts to expect, flow and BE-love, your mind will participate in your daily and creative life in an entirely new way.

Opening Up New Doorways To Abundance

Within your experience many of you lack much of what you desire in terms of material things, and the financial resources to choose and create lifestyle experiences, which you feel strongly would bring you happiness and peace.

In this transitioning time, it's important to begin to qualify your sense of lack by questioning how this relates to the innate Oneness you now know exists. You are challenged in this way because you are now ready to move up to higher levels. You know that in Oneness you are not separated from anything. Separation exists only as a mindset, an emotional and even a mental habit or pattern. Belief in or living from a perspective of separation makes experiencing financial and material abundance or prosperity difficult to impossible for many of you. You actually stop yourself from achieving it with your limited mindsets.

This Earth is not a place that simply caters to entitlement. Being *Lightworkers* does not mean that you suddenly become magnetic to things that are not a vibrational match to your emotional beliefs and patterns. You experience what is a match for your energy. You are not "rewarded " in life for being Lightworkers. The New Earth will not solve all of this by magically taking away the experience of money, nor by releasing you from the incredibly fun and joyful experience of aligning with that which you desire and discovering your POWER! That would be insulting to you and would impede your growth. And although you may say, "*No, Spirit, I would be relieved. Trust me-please just bring it on, that prosperity experience!*" It will not come into your experience in this way. Spirit or the Angels do not bring individuals money or material goods. The energy to do that is within YOU and comes as you drop your fears and align with the powerful energy of abundance. *Money comes to me and flows through me and back out to do the good.*

Now that the veil is lifted regarding these lingering illusions, let's explore wholeness and unity as it relates to money in some depth. You need to be reminded of ideas that you use to allow the true nature of reality to flow freely within your experience, to loosen up and release your fears, and bring in your amazing new higher-level energy.

First of all, you are free and powerful. You are one with All-That-Is. *You carry within you the energy and imprints of the entire universe*. Your soul vibration lives as

Backstage
The Importance of Your Personal
Inner Connection

a particularized aspect of Source Energy contained within the Unified Field. In the concept and focus of this spiritual energy you are embodied in your human life experience. To treat your life as though you cannot master this is to deny your innate Divinity!

Creating Money and tuning in to the *Keys to Abundance* on the Earth Plane is a shift, which you can experience most easily by taking small steps. The part of you that embraces and nurtures a scene in which there is a sudden shift and everything in your life in this way is immediately and suddenly resolved, is a debilitating intention for most of you. This thought process ironically puts an enormous amount of pressure on you, rather than improving your experience. Very few humans are able to align with such an enormous shift and change. It is far easier to make small changes, see movement, and grow with the learning; to be uplifted, inspired, and create again using this momentum.

You are now encouraged to claim your power, which for starters, means realizing if you are not yet experiencing material and financial abundance, and you wish to, then begin by considering how you might revise your understanding of your thoughts from, "It doesn't exists," or "In the new earth there won't be any money," to something a bit more accurate in our Universe, which is comprised entirely of energy: You are not yet a match or in harmony for what you desire, and your inner vibration has to grow and change to be more aligned with that which you seek.

You may have some new ideas of how to accomplish this. You may have heard things and tried things. But essentially, if you aren't living it, you don't yet consciously know how to get in sync with it. For starters, what if you realized this, with complete love and affection for yourself, and instead, begin to learn-remember-realize what needs to occur to get you in sync? What if you acknowledged, that no matter how old you are, how enlightened you are, how many lifetimes you've lived, how spiritual or "good" you are, that perhaps, there are some wonderful and amazing things you might need to learn or truthfully remember which would shift all of this financial stuff more toward abundance and what you'd enjoy?

Some of you are already learning and practicing, and those who are have had moments of insight, moments of suddenly having more money, or things come to them effortlessly and freely. They experience the floodgates opening when one comes into alignment with what they intend and create and watch it immediately come in to form. You people know what I mean. (See chapter 5)

Take a moment and listen directly— all those who are honestly, deeply tortured by financial experiences in their lives; those who are experiencing profound stress, self-hatred, and pain, based on their relationship to money: reflect on the fact that as a result, you often find yourself angry with those who charge money or seemingly "too much money" for that which you want. You feel critical and express negative energy to those who do this.

You find yourself looking at wealthy people and finding all kinds of things wrong with them. You can't yet see that YOU ARE THAT, with all those faults. You are the wealthy person. Innately. When you criticize them, you criticize you. Then, that part of you cannot come forth freely in your experience. It lurks in your shadow, angry and unexpressed. It comes forth in resentment toward those who are in the flow of prosperity or abundance to one degree or another. Instead of observing and noticing how these people live as a way of learning what, within their lives, might speak to you directly, while seeing how you might begin to live with a mindset more like theirs, you can't because you choose to create a separation between you and them. Be aware that in this separation, you also separate yourself from your own financial abundance.

Years ago there was a great teacher and writer, Yogananda, who taught that you were meant to experience *everything* which you were capable of appreciating. This is indeed true. This does not mean that since you have that potential, these experiences will flow to you without your coming into alignment with this truth. This again would rob you of your own power. You must go through the schooling, learning, and growth and adapt as you have your learning experiences.

Backstage
The Importance of Your Personal
Inner Connection

Now, take a deep breath, and let's refresh our memory as to what we've remembered together and celebrated about our beautiful Universe. For hasn't this opening experience revealed YOU and deepened your appreciation of some of the key themes of the Universe and indeed of the present human condition?

Unity—Harmony—Balance—Love—Oneness—
Multidimensional—Completion— Divinity.

All of these qualities are innately YOU. Many of you have experienced firsthand getting into sync with these qualities; allowing them to flow into all aspects of you and your experience. This has taken some major effort and has been physically, emotionally and mentally challenging. Opening your 8th Chakra will alleviate a lot of this tension. You have had to let go of a great deal, and realign several times to get there.

To an extent this is true with the quality of Prosperity. To claim the financial abundance—which is yours, you have to let go of issues/contrary ideas that you have with wealth; with wealthy people; with money; with charging money; with asking for money for your work. Many of you don't really like yourselves that much or acknowledge the valuable gifts you possess and give out to others. You don't realize that first of all money is just a form of energy. It's a resource. It's just energy and it flows and flows, and flows, into all kinds of situations and forms. Just like energy, sometimes it gets stuck and that creates a problem. Sometimes there is resistance to it and that creates more problems. As long as you trust it, use it, love it, play with it, and don't hold on, but open up to receive, allowing yourself to ask for it, want it, and let it flow freely without fear, it will work and flow just fine for you. However, you only receive as much as you think you deserve. And guess what? YOU decide what you deserve. Perhaps you ought to do some serious internal inquiry as to how much and why. (BTW You can muscle test for the amount your subconscious thinks you deserve.)

If you're not experiencing the prosperity you wish then you need to find the reason now, of why you feel you don't deserve it. The answer will likely come down to either not loving yourself enough and/or not believing you're enough just as you are, and/or thinking you have to "do" something to make it happen; that "something" is always out in the future. It's never now or here. Well all of this energy and these thoughts are getting you nowhere but unhappy.

Open up some doors by making peace with money and everything about it. Make this as important as making peace with Unity and Love and Oneness, as important as sending energy to heal the Gulf of Mexico or energetic support for the Earth. You react to these comments because there is still duality in your belief system. You still have some beliefs and patterns of living that are rooted in the concept of separateness and a lack of worthiness. Realize all the value judgment that still exists in your experience. There is a lot of it on Earth, and it will take some time, work, and doing to release the charge of it by including everything in your experience as something you can love and appreciate, and realizing you are not separate from wealth! Or anything!

So I ask you. May I please come forth and simply show you another way?

Backstage
The Importance of Your Personal
Inner Connection

NOTES:

Elizabeth Joyce

CHAPTER EIGHT
CREATING LONGLASTING ABUNDANCE
LIFETIME AFTER LIFETIME

Just for starters—let's be beginners. You've just met money for the first time. It is being shown to you. Look! Here is this amazing energy form, which you can use to create things in your life! You can use it to pay for lumber for your new doghouse. You can use it to buy a pizza. You can use it to create labels for your new essential healing oils. You can use it to buy a new computer monitor so you can write without your eyes getting tired. You can use it to pay for special surgery so you can open your eyes and read a book or see clearly again.

Now, let's consider the other side of the money game What would you like to do and be during the day? Do you want to read? Talk to people? Make things with your hands? Create rituals? Play with your kids? Would you like to learn how to create pastries? How to advise people on making career changes? To help and support people as they prepare to die?

Whatever you would enjoy learning, being, doing, imagine that being a way you receive money, if you'd like to receive money from this. If not, imagine how you'd like to receive money. But be careful here-take small steps and don't violate other people's free choice. For example, decide what you'd like to do for work and if it's with others in an organized setting, then ask to be guided to it and pay attention. Get the word out that you have this interest. Look for job openings on the computer. Update your resume. You have to take an action to bring in a result. What goes around comes around, as they say. Tell people you know what you're looking for. Expect it to show up. Find ways to start living and being in that mode already. Begin to thank Spirit for your new, fabulous job. In your meditation, list what the new job has brought to you. Perfect remuneration, wonderful people to work with, an easy to get to office, recognition for your talents. Allow yourself to feel as if you have the job already.

Tell money you love it. If you don't love it, you're disconnected from money somehow. All forms of separation in thinking and behavior limit your innate divine creative power. Money is an energy, which allows you to exchange, affirm, and create experiences you value. Money is another way you express appreciation for that which you value and which gives you joy: like that beautiful haircut which makes you feel so handsome, or that spa treatment that turns all of your muscles into noodles, or that dinner with your daughter to celebrate her piano recital and treat her to a luxurious experience as she enters young adult hood. Or that animal shelter, which helps to find homes for dogs that you love. Money helps you create in the world. It's energy. Just like focus. Just like attention. It's just energy. The money you have is the energy you have.

For starters, make peace with money. Then make peace with people who make money. Make peace with people who charge money. And really, really, really, make peace with people who make *lots and lots* of money because it shows you that it's an option if you want it. Be appreciative for the idea that it exists. Begin to see if you can embrace the mindset of someone who has money. Be aware that money brings the freedom to make choices, to do things, to create things, to have experiences, to live with ease and focus on creating and expressing, on loving and learning, on understanding and thinking, inventing and transforming while knowing aliveness. It brings the sense of expecting to have the ability to choose freely, more and more to your lifestyle.

Take this seriously and begin your inner work. Accept that learning to master the keys to prosperity, and releasing all that stands in your way, is going to be your focus for a while, as it ought to be in order to get yourself to a place where that part of life is ironed out a bit. This is important for it will give you a platform that you desire, from which to create and express yourself. Let go of any negative aspects and false beliefs you have held toward money in the past.

The size of this energy flow will vary. Some prefer more some prefer less. But most of you are still learning how to allow in what you prefer. And that is what I'd like you to claim as the next theme for 2020 that you will master.

Following is a new mantra that is used at the National Council of Churches in New York City:

Money comes to me
And flows through me
And back out to do the good.

Know that Unity, Balance, Harmony, Oneness, Love, Alignment, Expansion, Multidimensionality and most important, Divinity, are all extended by Prosperity and Wealth. The other part of balance, which is necessary, is mental, emotional, and physical health and wellbeing. If you can radically accept this form of exchange as a part of you and your creativity, then you will never suffer from greed and wanting to hurt others because of money. It will come in, flow, and become a natural part of you. You will have all that you need.

Let's take a look backstage again to see and understand how this works:

My son Jeffrey graduated from High School in 1983. He was in the top 98% of the country and aced his SAT's easily. I knew he had caught the brains of the family genes. He had to go to college, as well as a good, accredited school. His father disagreed with me and wanted Jeffrey to go to the local Community College. He claimed he could not afford to send Jeffrey to any sort of good school.

His father was a pharmacist and earned a very good salary. Although I worked in aviation at Teterboro Airport,

67

as an assistant to the Ground Services Manager, my annual salary was two-thirds less than his. Yet, I was determined to make this work.

We began the college search early in the fall of his senior year because I knew I needed "mind time" to get up the energy to pay the bills. I told him we had to make an early decision if possible. We lived in Northern New Jersey just outside of New York City, and had a nice list of schools to choose from. I had heard of Lehigh University from some of my high school classmates, and wanted to check that one out. We stayed away from Ivy League schools because of the expense.

I want to address this here. I would never put myself, or my family into a threatening position by over-extending ambition. I would not put us, knowingly, into financial distress. This is a part of integrity. I knew that I could take his father to court to get more funds for college, but what good would that do? It would cost more to do that than perhaps a year of college, and to me that would be a waste. So Ivy League colleges were out.

Jeffrey interviewed well at several schools. We had a few offers but Lehigh offered Jeffery a scholarship as well as an early decision. It was a done deal.

Okay, so now what? I had until June to raise the funds for the first year. I had to go deep within and make a visual plan to do so. I took a job in Adult School teaching self-hypnosis and developing your psychic sensitivity. I began reading tarot cards at the local Psychic Fair on Sundays. I also took on some small accounting jobs, such as payroll and other bookwork. (Remember, we had no computers then.) I told Jeffrey that I would not be home much, and the family provided him with his first car, a sliver Honda Civic. Jeffrey had a part time job at the local pharmacy, and we began to work together toward the Lehigh goal

Let me show you what props came out from backstage once the decisions were made.

Jeffrey was awarded a Pell Grant from the government. I received a nice raise at the airport. My table was packed on Sundays for readings, and I had more than full classes at the Adult School. This is known as *being supported by the Universe*. We made it through that first year, and every other year became easier. With his grades, he advanced, got more scholarships, and became a Gryphon (to manage the dorm) for his dorm. That paid for his housing and meals.

What was the payoff for this dedication to a project and such hard work? Jeffrey graduated Magna Cum Laude and then went into Rutgers College of Medicine. He is now an ophthalmologist in Ramsey, New Jersey.

Do you see? The New Human is emerging in a way you perhaps did not anticipate. Ascension is not a one-moment event. Ascension happens continually. It's an *ascending energy arc* you want to be riding on, living on, attuned with, as often as possible. Pick up the energy *Backstage*, and direct it to achieving your goals and desires in life. Then, all the rest will follow.

The *New Multi-Dimensional Human* has resolved the duality of the past. In the past, spiritual pursuits were not very integrated with mastering commerce and money. Now the corporations are becoming consciously aware for their employees. In that sense, the old loyalty ways of the 1950-60's are coming back into form on a higher scale.

Spirituality was pursued as though it was separate from money, and Religion was often the path, and that became separate from any concept of energy. So much of the old paradigms involved separating things; sex from holiness, money from spirituality, goodness from financial aspirations. All of these old paradigms were based on separateness.

In this millennium we're all about *oneness,* inclusiveness, and unity. Not because we think these are *nice ideas*, but because we know that *reality is one interconnected, expanding, diversifying energetic field*. So let's get on with mastering that which will allow each of you beautiful beings to diversify the Universe with specificity, which is yours alone! That's your role here, to create newness!

The new human might meditate, get a facial, work with homeless people, live in a city, be divorced, channel angels, have memories of being abducted on a spaceship for upgrades. Teaching the new human is as diverse, beautiful, complex, and unique as the Earth is.

All the ways you hoped Ascension would remove things that you have not yet mastered is also an old paradigm, which says that you don't have power and need to be rescued by something. Ascension is not about rescuing you. It's about each of you finding your own limitless point of creativity and alignment and flowing with it, inspiring others by your example, activating their codes with your Light expansion, and collectively creating phenomenal, already unstoppable momentum. This Fifth Dimension Double Helix, amber energy is something you create. It's entirely about *your amazing power*. Finding it, flowing with it, and enjoying it. Ascension is about Unity. The entire experience is about a club, which welcomes everyone, everything and all ways of doing it.

This is a lot to get your head around, isn't it? That's why you have a heart. It opens and lets everything in, very naturally. The Heart is made for Love.

The ascending energy will take you everywhere you want to go, but you've got to work and flow with it. You need to let it surface and resolve past issues within you to clear the way for the new, really fabulous experiences. You have to welcome it. Radically!

Ascension isn't going to override your own belief system. Your belief system will simply weigh down the arc a bit, and you'll look up to see people riding high like you'd like. You can join them at any time if that's your preference. Just throw a few things out of your black bag.

Lighten the load people. This new life is all yours anyway, in this amazing, endless wholeness.

CHAPTER NINE

OPENING THE DIMENSIONAL DOORWAYS

Tools for Opening Dimensional Doorways

1. Create Your Personal Vortex:
Understand that energy is always in motion. The infinite
energy known as Chi, Shakti, or the Amber/Gold Light (in
the new language) is energy that moves in a circular
motion, clockwise, having no beginning and no end. Your
expression of this energy is to place it in finite form and see
if you can hold your power in that form. This circle needs
to connect with both of the heart chakras, the 4th and the 10th.
Therefore begin to spin in a circular motion to set up your
own personal energy vortex. Experience this in any fashion
that works for you.

Go inside and discover the manner in which to
facilitate these personal energy fields. Begin with
projecting an amber/yellow stream of Light through the 4th
Heart Chakra; pull this streaming light energy out through
your spine and see it rise up to the 10th Chakra. Then feel
this light stream drop down the front of your body to the 4th
Heart Center. Sense the beaming golden yellow Light
flowing into your lower heart chakra, out your spine, and
rising up to meet with the 10th Chakra, the new Heart
Center, and back down again into the 4th Chakra—the heart
center.

Anything can be healed in this powerful Circle of Light. All that is needed will be unveiled to you; any relationship can be balanced and healed. Find a way to create circular energy fields around yourselves, by visualizing the new fourth level of the Aura wrapping around your entire energetic field, including the new Spiritual Chakras. This will facilitate the changes that you now face and bring them about in very positive, healthy ways.

2. Collective Intentional Vortices

Creating a vortex within a group also makes space for them in your lives as you interact with the Earth on a collective basis. In a large or small group you can create a vortex of energy moving in a circle, which is always flowing clockwise. Decide what area of the body to focus on to make these circles of Light, as a collective connection to the Earth and work with her to create a vortex. Unlike personal vortices, once a collective vortex is placed into motion, it remains in that spot. These funnels will be used by the Earth to anchor and distribute the Amber, pure energy onto the planet. (It's like the energy of the Holy Ghost or higher Shakti energy) Later, some of these same energy fields will turn into the portals that will be used to travel between dimensional realities.

3. Turn Right.

The door between realities is one of a right angle. Oneness-Fifth Dimensional reality is separated from another by ninety degrees. Begin to use this intention to change the course of your own life experience.

In those instances when you find your reality not to your liking, stop and turn ninety degrees from where you are. Again you must turn in a clockwise direction. Trust yourselves to know this. Do this first as a tool of symbolic gesture and soon you will understand the true use of this Universal truth—*Living On Light.*

4. The Creation of the Lightbody.

On December 21, 2012 the planet was gifted with a new, stronger and higher frequency Light Ray. Known as the *Double Helix*, it flows onto the planet from the center of our galaxy. This fulfills the promise of this date, and had been anticipated to arrive on our planet for Eons. This Amber Gold frequency is extremely powerful and can transform any darkness into Light in a flash. It uplifts, heals, removes energy blocks, and opens one up to be in alignment with the flow of the universe, without thought or struggle. Everything on the planet is undergoing transformation under these rays. That is what is meant by the expression, *destruction before reconstruction.*

While the planet is undergoing a shift to a higher frequency, because she is a living moving energy system, all who reside within her energy fields will also experience this realignment. Consequently MENTOR has sent through a description of the process, in detail:

First: what many are experiencing naturally as the planet undergoes her transformation, is termed the *Creation of the Lightbody.*

Following is an outline of the different stages we may experience as this occurs and how it is manifesting in your own energy fields e.g. bouts of flu, headaches etc. (This is discussed in detail in my Ascension Workbook.)

Second: as many are enthusiastic and joyous about these changes, it's important to cover practical things that we can consciously do to build and increase the Light quotient in our own bodies.

Tuning ourselves into the higher octaves of Light and changing our vibrational frequency is a process, and may not be easy for a lot of you. Following are a few additional techniques to accelerate this process. *The process of transition into Light is a gradual one.* We are not matter one day and pure Light the next. Our energy fields are infused with and realigned to Light gradually or else we would experience *electrical burn out.*

The entire crystalline structure of matter was activated only to the 3rd level Lightbody, for all planetary inhabitants, in August, 1987 at the Harmonic Convergence. The necessary creation of the Lightbody is due to the planet's current transition process and is not an optional experience or process.

Backstage
The Importance of Your Personal
Inner Connection

Beings not wishing to be part of this process will choose death by accident, natural disaster, or decay and disease. It is foretold that they will continue their cycle of evolution on another planet of frequency comparable to their own - there is no judgment - it is just the changing nature of energy. The Lightbody is gradually created through the transmutation of our current physical body as it receives and absorbs more Light. This is interconnected with the realignment of our energy fields to higher frequencies and higher octaves of Light. This process will activate the *Soul's DNA* for the first time ever on this planet.

The following information describes the actual physical process and common physical symptoms as this change occurs. We are all evolving and absorbing Light at our own pace. Some are consciously working with these changes and their transmutation is quicker, some are unaware and are absorbing this Light and change in direct relation to planetary change. However, one can classify this expansion as growth of the human body into higher levels:

First level - when the body drops density it commonly displays mutational symptoms of flu, headaches, diarrhea, rashes, muscle and joint aches. Most flu epidemics are actually Light epidemics. Brain chemistry changes, right and left brain functions blend and the pituitary and pineal glands begin to change in size. The DNA structure and chemical components begin to change and pick up extra hydrogen atoms and chemicals that the cells need to take undifferentiated higher Light and break it down into useable Light codes for the DNA.

Second level - the etheric blueprint floods with light and releases karmic experiences, individuals may feel disoriented as well as experience 'bouts of flu'. Many begin to question "why am I here". Light in the etheric blueprint releases 4th dimensional structure vibrations and causes spins in the geometries of the emotional, mental and spiritual bodies. Change is rapid and many feel extremely tired. If you need to lay down in the middle of the day, be

74

sure to do so. This allows the invisible forces and beings to work on you and your adapting to your personal ascension.

Third level – the physical senses become much stronger. Your body not only absorbs Light for its own change, but also, acts as a transducer—decoder of higher Light energies to the planet as a whole. The process of the in-breath is now irreversible, like an elastic band that has been stretched to maximum capacity, has been let go of and snaps back, returning to its natural Soul state before birth.

Fourth level - major chemical changes are happening in the brain and its chemistry and electromagnetic energy symptoms are often expressed as headaches, blurry vision, loss of hearing, and sometimes chest pains. Crystal regulators in the etheric body, in the 8 ½ Chakra, keep lines of light within the 5th dimensional blueprint from connecting again until you are ready.

Chest pains are due to the expanding energies of the heart as it opens to wider and deeper levels. Vision and hearing are being realigned to function differently. The mental body begins to wonder if it really is in charge and individuals get strong unexplainable and undeniable urges to follow Spirit without hesitation. Individuals may get flashes of telepathy, clairvoyance, and also begin to experience a deeper empathy. This is a time of feeling, of honoring, accepting, and validating the emotional body and learning to work with the new energies in order to control them in a down to Earth fashion.

Fifth level - the mental body decides to tune to spirit by meditation or other means. Dreams change and may become more 'lucid'; you get feelings of *de ja vu*. Thought processes become non linear. Beings oscillate between knowing and doubt. We realize the habitual nature of thinking and behavior. We begin to look at and work with de-programming and re-programming to create the "I" we wish to be, not the "I" we thought we were from our interaction with parents, peers and society. Change seems to be constant and we consciously begin to discern from our heart rather than to make decisions or judge from *conditioned responses*.

Sixth level - we draw to us others who are going through this process, for mutual support and stimulation of growth. We question what is real, our mental process, and how we identify with others and ourselves; everything seem to change rapidly. Self-examination and re-evaluation may be uncomfortable but we feel it must be done. We look at our relationships, jobs, home environment, lifestyles; it may be a time of letting go, of moving on. We change our friends, everything feels to be in a state of flux, but we feel lighter, vaster, and freer somehow. By this stage the Light quotient in our being is at least 33% - we feel as though we are opening up our inner senses and clairvoyance, clairaudience, and intuitive gifts. This all seems normal and natural to us.

Seventh level - the Heart Chakra has reversed colors with the Solar Plexux, becoming a bright yellow light, opens more, and we become in touch and more honest with other emotions; with a stronger sense of self-esteem, we allow ourselves to bring forth the true *inner Self*. We release blocks and old patterns—it brings a time of great emotional clearing and focused intensity as we seek to rid ourselves of outdated emotional baggage. We feel more in tune with each moment, allowing our Selves to feel very present and flowing with life.

Often old relationships end or change rapidly as beings dig deep and honor their feelings - there is simply no room for denial on any level. We begin to lose our emotional attachments to others. Chest pains (angina) are more common as the heart continues to open its energy fields. (Doing the *Chakras and Your Body* or *Opening The 8th Chakra* meditation will assist in the heart opening).

Fear at this time, is released as the energy fields of all the bodies are realigned through the heart center and when the 4th Chakra and 10th Chakra are aligned, fear drops away. Pressure at the forehead or back or the head is due to the opening of the 9th Chakra as well as the pituitary and pineal glands as they absorb more light. When these glands are fully open, activated, and functioning at the highest level, aging and death cease. Be aware that this can take several years.

When the pineal gland is fully open we experience multi-dimensionality, yet a sense of duality seems to increase as we leave it behind. Some days we feel connected and joyous, others we are in fear and caught up in survival issues. Many wish to *ascend and leave the planet* as we sense the very real possibility of ascension through our deepening connection with Spirit. As we learn to follow our joy, we may then begin to want to save the planet and have everyone follow the joy.

ALL are stages of progression and reflect our changing perception. Dietary wise, you want to eat less, more light, freshly grown food. Many at this stage have ceased to eat meat, sugar, or drink alcohol as they feel the effects of these substances on the vibrational fields of the body as uncomfortable. They may have a sense of shutting down as well.

Eighth level - We see our divine Masters in all we do and purely wish to be of service as we leave the saving and rescuing mode behind in favor of the desire to serve *Divine Will.* The pineal and pituitary glands change shape, becoming more attached to the 6th Chakra of pure vision. If headaches persist, ask the Beings and Guides who are working with you to simply *tone it down* so they don't feel pain, or ask them to release endorphins—the brains natural opiate. The brain is being activated on a higher level, particularly the cerebrum, the brain's *sleeping giant.*

Cranial expansion is common; triangular seed crystals in the brow ridge, and recorder crystals in the right side of the brain are activated along with the 8th, 9th and 10th Chakras. We begin to be tethered to the new *languages of Light.*

The pituitary and pineal glands are opened fully and work together to create the natural and etheric *Arc of the Covenant,* a rainbow of light that emits from the 9th Chakra and arcs over the top of the head to the third eye chakra that is a decoding mechanism for higher dimensional language.

You may find it hard to find words to express yourself as you may think in geometries and tones. If confused do the chakra meditation and ask for messages to be decoded and translated.

Again you become much more aware of the
vastness and multi-dimensionality of the Universe and your
nature. You *Know* you can be anything that you want to be,
you cease to operate from obligation and relationships
become transpersonal. You share words from your higher
heart and soul and others may feel disorientated when
dealing with you, as they no longer have tethers into you to
hook on to. You operate from a deep level of serenity with
heightened sensitivity and awareness yet feel grounded and
transformed. By this stage, it is possible to be sustained
purely by Light and prana, (the breath), to take nourishment
from the atmospheric realms and to be healthily sustained
by the etheric. However, water is very important at this
level and you must continue to hydrate.

Ninth level - decoding geometries and toning is
easier. Spirit is using the *language of light,* which shifts the
5th dimensional blueprint into a new template for your 5th
dimensional Lightbody. Your body may change shape as
the energy fields shift. You feel interconnected to all
Beings everywhere and less connected to the opinions of
others.

You release the desire for and the energy to sustain
the *game of separation and limitatio*n and feel truly free.
The 9th level sees a mass dissension of the Lightbody into
physical form. As with the 3rd and 6th, this level sees a
strong re-evaluation as we begin the *final surrender to
Spirit* and we truly become a Divine instrument. Here Spirit
determines our income, our work, other beings who come
into our life, everything. This is the dissolution of the ego-
self and while ecstatic, it can be most painful. Making the
leap can be fearful even though we have worked hard to
evolve through eons of lifetimes to reach this point. We
may go back and forth, clinging to old comfort zones
before completely letting go. However, there is really no
turning back and all past karma and tethers must be
released.

The 9th level is surrender and then ecstasy; it's the
letting go of the "I". We fully understand that while free
will is real, it's also an illusion as it's only there to guide us
and to empower us to be One with Spirit. Survival fears

78

leave and the focus is on the Now at-one-ment. Though fears may surface, they seem unreal and are easily put aside. We tend to disconnect from consensus reality and our choices in our new reality seem unreal to others.

From the 7th, 8th and 9th Levels the inner light noticeably radiates out and by now you feel unbelievably grounded, connected, centered, filled with purpose, desiring only to serve.

For a while you may slip between the Eighth and Ninth Levels, from feeling complete at-one-ment to being a limited human being again. This duality feeling settles down by the end of the ninth level. At that time you continually feel connected and operate from your Soul Master energies level. Your intention and motivation is always for the highest, although others, due to their own inner triggers and issues, may not always choose or be able to see that. The Ninth Level is where the 9th Chakra begins to open as we begin to hook up to our I AM awareness. The last three levels unify all energy fields, all chakras are unified, and you become totally connected to your I AM Self or the Blessed Higher Self. Your Lightbody and your physical body have become one.

Tenth level – You have pierced the Astral Plane and are now receiving your Light Ray from the Universal Consciousness in the unlimited universe. You are one with Source consciousness and know all is possible. DNA is no longer two strands but twelve strands; telepathy, teleportation, manifestation, are instantaneous. The Merkabah grid has been built and allows you to pass through space, time, and dimensions, complete in your totality. It has its own consciousness and is co-directed by you.

Eleventh level - all levels of the Lightbody have been constructed and activated and are connected to your physical body via their *spin points*. These light matrix's lie along the physical acupuncture meridians of the body and are lines of light intersecting in beautiful geometrics. A new 5th dimensional circulatory system of Light, causing cellular regeneration, has been activated.. Time is no longer linear but simultaneous; past, present and future co-exist. All life experiences exist in parallels. There is no separation

79

and you will fully manifest your vision of Heaven on Earth, and express the ecstasy of Spirit.

In this realm of conscious awareness, many now access and create new types of Light based technologies, new community living, new systems of government and equitable food and resource distribution systems. All have received specialist training and their skills have been brought forth to help create and manifest *the New World; the Golden Age*.

Twelfth level - the continuation of the Creation and implementation of the New World systems. You will now hook up with other 12th level initiates who bring into existence new governments, new financial and educational systems, a better system of food and resource allocation, as all will be redefined in the final stages of Earth's ascension so that all may exist in joy, equality and harmony. By this time the planet and her inhabitants will have been rewoven into Light to shine in their full glory as the final stages of this Divine Plan unfolds. The planet goes to Light, shifts out of this lower level, dark dimension, and is brought into a multi-star system where everyone is a Lightbody and follows Spirit in total Mastery. All parallel realities are rewoven and absorbed back to Spirit and all have aligned their will to be joined and interwoven with the Divine.

CHAPTER TEN

THS DNA OF THE SOUL

Teach the secrets, wisdom, knowledge,
And practices of the Soul.
So that all can do Soul healing
For the physical, mental, emotional,
And spiritual bodies.
These are the keys to the New World.

— Mentor

A human being has a soul, mind, and body. Your mind can do a lot for your life, and becomes stronger when it aligns with the heart. The mind can:

Heal the body
Transform consciousness
Create and manifest
Connect with the heart to become even more powerful

These are examples of mind over matter. There has been a great deal of scientific research and demonstrations of the power of the mind. Think of Uri Geller's ability to bend spoons and move objects. We recognize and accept the power of the mind. However, this power is not enough.

The next step to Soul Growth is to have a desire to serve humanity. *Soul over matter* is the way to create and make things happen is a positive way in your life. This includes:

Backstage
The Importance of Your Personal
Inner Connection

Prevention of sickness
Soul healing (beyond the body)
Soul Grace, the lifting of karma
Soul energy lengthening your life span
Soul transformation in every aspect of life

The final power of the Soul is to enlighten all souls of humanity as well as all souls in all areas of the universe. This new energy, the fifth dimension double helix energy, is the energy for soul growth.

In the new millennium of the 21ˢᵗ Century mankind has moved from mind over matter to *soul over matter*. This new Soul Light Era is a marvelous turning point for humanity. As we move along through the decades, many Light workers will be empowered to be a part of the transformation of people's views, transform every occupation, transform relationships within the family structures, as well as receive remarkable results for healing all forms of life.

As people meditate, connect with and join this Divine energy, workshops, teleconferences, radio programs movies, and TV shows will confirm this power. The Divine has downloaded the information needed as well as healing power to thousands of Light workers. Hundreds of healers have created and assisted in remarkable results for healing.

The Divine has created hundreds of writers in the last twenty years, giving us Divine Books which are inspiring while opening the hearts of the readers. Books are coming out in a flowing stream, one right after the other. Their information, while similar, covers thousands of spiritual subjects to help and guide people in all walks of life.

To add to all this, the Diving has dropped down a lot of energy for Grace, which brings us karma cleansings, which is explained in the next chapter. Soul Power is the gift of the twenty-first century. By applying the varied techniques to bring in and enhance your Soul Power, you can completely transform your thinking, raise your vibration, help with prevention of sickness, recalibration, prolong life, soul transformation, and embrace enlightenment. Along with the rest of humanity, your view of the world can be completely transformed, bringing in the Golden Era of love, peace, and harmony.

(Working with *the New Spiritual Chakras* will speed up this process and tightly connect you with the invisible Divine energy; the amber light, double-helix energy of the Fifth Dimension.)

It has been taught that one cannot create or manifest Grace. Only God can give us Grace, or a fully realized Saint, such as Mata Amritanandamayi. One can pray for Grace, or the lifting of Karma, but no one can "make it happen." It is always by the will of the Divine. However, at this time some Light workers are receiving the stream of Light energy to lift karma. These people are very few in number and if you happen to run across any one of them, you are very blessed. Just know that it has taken many, many lifetimes to have that experience.

"There are two types of education: one for living and one for life. To live life beneficially is what spirituality is all about. One should live beneficially both for society and for oneself. That's what spirituality is in its essence."
                                        — Hare Krishna

DNA is a multi- dimensional, crystalline structure that carries your unique energetic "imprint" and "history" across lifetimes. (This is soul-level view of DNA — a very different understanding than your college biology books). Your Soul DNA is far beyond the "biological DNA" acquired from your birth parents.

The fact is that DNA was separated through the separation of the spiritual reality and the physical reality. That jolt gave humankind only two strands of DNA, when in actuality, there are 12 strands. The body and soul are supposed to be one unit, one reality. What we don't see is just as real as what we do see, and soon we will learn to see it all. That is what is known as ascension.

Your complete DNA is an energetic signature that transcends the need for the body. You've already reached a greater level of awareness through your five senses – this is your soul transcending materiality. Now we are moving beyond the sixth sense up to the reality of the twelfth sense. This ascension will take many years to achieve, and perhaps many lifetimes.

The reality of the soul is among the most important questions of life. Although religions go on and on about its existence, how do we know if souls really exist?

The idea of the soul is bound up with the Law of Karma, the idea of a future life and our belief in a continued existence after death. It's said to be the ultimate principle by which we think and feel, but isn't dependent on the body. In fact it's believed by many that the soul is separate from the body. Many infer the soul's existence without scientific analysis or reflection. Indeed, the mysteries of birth and death, the play of consciousness during dreams – such as imagination and memory – suggest the existence of a vital life force that exists independent of the body.

However, the current scientific thinking system doesn't recognize this spiritual dimension of life. We're told we're just the activity of carbon and some proteins; we live awhile and then die: as for the Universe? It too has no meaning. It has all been worked out in mathematical equations – no need for a soul.

But now biocentrism – *a new theory of everything* – challenges this traditional, materialistic idea of reality. In all research directions, this outdated paradigm leads to insoluble enigmas, to ideas that are ultimately irrational. But knowledge and new ideas are the prelude to wisdom, and soon our worldview will catch up with the facts.

Of course, most spiritual people view the soul as emphatically more definitive than the scientific concept. It's considered the invisible but living essence of a person, and is said to be immortal and transcendent of material existence. But when scientists speak of the soul (if at all), it's usually in a materialistic context, or treated as a poetic synonym for the mind: They expound that, "Everything knowable about the 'soul' can be learned by studying the functioning of the brain". In their view, neuroscience is the only branch of scientific study relevant to understanding the soul.

Traditionally, science has dismissed the soul as an object of human belief, or reduced it to a psychological concept that shapes our idea of the observable natural world. The terms "life" and "death" are thus nothing more than the common concepts of "biological life" and "biological death." The animating principle is simply the laws of chemistry and physics. You (and all the poets and philosophers that ever lived) are just ashes and dust orbiting the core of the Milky Way galaxy.

As one researches most of the scientific books, you can't find a single reference to the soul, or any notion of an immaterial, eternal essence that occupies our being. Indeed, a soul has never been seen under an electron microscope, nor spun in the laboratory in a test tube or ultra-centrifuge. According to these books, nothing appears to survive the human body after death.

While neuroscience has made tremendous progress illuminating the functioning of the brain, why we have a subjective experience remains mysterious. The problem of the soul lies exactly here, in understanding the nature of the self, the "I" in existence that feels and lives life. But this isn't just a problem for biology and cognitive science, but for the entire nature of Western philosophy itself.

The current worldview – the world of objectivity and naïve realism – is beginning to show some fatal cracks. Of course, this will not surprise many of the philosophers and other readers who, contemplating the works of men such as Plato, Socrates and Kant, and of Buddha and other great spiritual teachers, kept wondering about the relationship between the universe and the mind of man. But what about the "out-of-body experience or NDE reports? How can that be explained in a logical and scientific way?

Recently, biocentrism and other scientific theories have started to challenge the old physico-chemical paradigm, and to ask some of the difficult questions about life: Is there a soul? Does anything endure the ravages of time?

Life and consciousness are central to this new view of being, reality as well as the cosmos. Although the current scientific paradigm is based on the belief that the world has an objective observer-independent existence, real experiments suggest just the opposite. We think life is just the activity of atoms and particles, which spin around for a while and then dissipate into nothingness. But if we add the life vibration waves to the equation, we can explain some of the major puzzles of modern science, including the uncertainty principle, entanglement, and the fine-tuning of the laws that shape the universe.

Consider the famous two-slit experiment. When you watch a particle go through the holes, it behaves like a bullet, passing through one slit or the other. But if no one observes the particle, it exhibits the behavior of a wave and can pass through both slits at the same time. This and other experiments tell us that unobserved particles exist only as 'waves of probability'. They're statistical predictions – nothing but a likely outcome. Until observed, they have no real existence; only when the mind sets the scaffolding in place, can they be thought of as having duration or a position in space. These experiments make it increasingly clear that even *mere knowledge in the experimenter's mind* is sufficient to convert the soul's possibility to a definite reality.

Many scientists dismiss the implications of these experiments, because until recently, this observer-dependent behavior was thought to be confined to the subatomic world; however, this idea is being challenged by researchers around the world. In fact, just this year a team of physicists showed that quantum weirdness also occurs in the human-scale world. They studied huge compounds composed of up to 430 atoms, and confirmed that this strange quantum behavior extends into the larger world we live in.

Most important, this has a direct bearing on the question of whether humans and other living creatures have souls. As Kant pointed out over 200 years ago, everything we experience – including all the colors, sensations, and objects we perceive – are nothing but representations in our mind. Space and time are simply the mind's tools for putting it all together. Now, to the amusement of idealists, scientists are beginning dimly to recognize that those rules make existence itself possible. Indeed, the experiments above suggest that objects only exist with real properties if they are observed. The results not only defy our classical intuition, but suggest that a part of the mind – the soul– is immortal and exists outside of space and time. (The mind is within the Soul, not visa versa.)

I have a suspicion that the DNA double helix form is a result of the union of the soul and the spirit. Spirit, on its own, is represented by RNA; on its own, it cannot replicate or create physical matter. But when a soul combines with spirit RNA, DNA is formed and thus replication can occur. Thus, according to this theory, *everything that has DNA has a soul* (bacteria, plants, trees, fungi, mitochondria, animals, etc).

Spirits, viral, supernatural, or otherwise, consists of only RNA. Thus, much like how viruses operate, spirits operate in the same manner. In order for them to take physical form and replicate, they need to combine with a soul.

Backstage
The Importance of Your Personal
Inner Connection

As humans, we have a soul and a spirit. But what we do, think, and feel have an impact on how well our soul is connected to our spirit. When the connection is weak, it gives room for a virus or spirits to " attack" or obtain a host. Once they combine with our DNA, they act like epigenetic factors, affecting DNA expression, and can even be passed down to future generations. Whether the effects are good or bad is subjective here. Sometimes disease happens, and sometimes mutations happen that allow for better adaptation to the environment. What determines an advantageous union from a disadvantageous one is how the soul processes the invasion, or how the soul is able to adapt itself to a symbiotic relationship. (See, "Psychic Attack, Are You A Victim?")

To reach Soul Enlightenment, which is a bit different from Self-Realization, or to change your vibration and ascend to higher levels of vibration, you need to uplift your soul standing in the Universe. This can only be accomplished by the development of character. The one thing you do take with you when you die is your character. This is your inner essence or vibrational force, containing the imprints of what you have learned and absorbed in the current lifetime. The higher the spiritual standing that you achieve in the current lifetime, the greater the blessings that can be received. These blessings include abilities to heal and transform your life as well as the ability to help and serve others.

All human beings have a soul. As the soul advances and uplift's its soul standing, through living life and reincarnation, the greater blessings can be received. Different souls vibrate at different levels, of which there are twelve. Only through the Law of Grace and service can one uplift its soul standing. A soul must go through hundreds of lifetimes improving its level, and can be uplifted higher and higher. If a soul chooses to live a mean-spirited or darkened lifetime, then its spiritual standing will descend.

Who makes this determination about whether a soul's spiritual standing should be uplifted or kept the same? It's in your Akashic Records, which are reviewed at the end of each lifetime. They are reviewed by the "Board of Nine," in the soul pod from where you descended and hosted your body in the lifetime you just exited. You go through the "Life Review", process the information, and then are placed in whatever vibration level you achieved in your most current lifetime. You will sense and feel every hurt you endured from that energy as well as who caused the pain. Then you will review every mean and low energy act you gave out, and also "see" the backstage effect: How you affected another's person's life and that outcome as well as what happened to you. This review brings you the "stamp of karma", that is energy put into your soul field to be relived and undone in your next lifetime.

After all is said and done, you begin to set up your astrological chart for the next lifetime, highlighting those issues that are not yet healed within your soul. There are different areas and different categories to work on. Therefore, a soul's journey is a long, long one. It can take hundreds of lifetimes to uplift your soul to a new level. If you are able to move on to a higher soul pod in one lifetime, you lived a lifetime well spent.

In your physical life, if you have good health, a good family, good love relationships, with good productivity and finances, then you are blessed. You are satisfied and at peace. You have inner joy and are able to help and serve others. You are enlightened.

The sooner your soul can reach a place of enlightenment, the sooner you can receive the special blessings from the Divine that go beyond the body; natural healing, strong intuition, devotion and telepathic abilities.

Backstage
The Importance of Your Personal Inner Connection

Your service must be unconditional. Study the lives of the masters, the holy saints, Buddha, and your spiritual teachers. Every one of them went through major spiritual testing. They were tested in lifetime after lifetime. No pain, no gain? No tests, no soul growth.

Begin now.

Make a vow and then a statement to God and the Universe.

I lovingly walk the path of love, peace, and harmony, allowing my energy to be directed by the Divine. May it be Thy will, not my will.

Your Statement of Truth:

I know who I am	A child of the universe
I know what I am	A living soul hosting a body
I know how I serve.	Using my natural abilities under the guidance of the Divine.

Tell the Universe you want to make a commitment to serve all of humanity and the entire Universe.

Setting a condition with the Divine is how we manifest our desires.

CHAPTER ELEVEN

THE POWER OF KARMA

Always, in the backstage of our life
The Universe in vibrating and moving
To bring to us that which we desire.
The energy happens before the action.
Therefore,

Everything we experience
We have brought into our reality.
It's humbling to know
That we all can bring to ourselves
Wonderful and *Unlimited Realities*.

—EAJ   3/26/2020

Our Soul's karma is the root cause of success or failure in every area of our life. Everyone's success depends on their service in past lives. Everyone's blockages are due to their mean-spirited or fearful actions in this lifetime as well as previous lifetimes. Be aware that your sibling, parent, and ancestor karma will also affect your present lifetime.

There are many great stories in history that show us that karma is the root cause of success and failure in every part of this present lifetime. I studied natural healing with Louise Hay and Indira Ivie of the Clear Light Group. However, it wasn't until I had my own healing practice that I realized the fact of "root cause". It was difficult for me to wrap my head around the fact that "every thought is a living and moving vibration", and that "what you think is what you get". The mysterious part is that most of our thoughts are in the subconscious and we are not aware of them or their power.

Grammie Hemphill taught me early on that everything we do, say, or think is "written down" or "recorded" in the universe. I couldn't believe that at the time. I actually though the angels would run out of paper. I knew nothing of a soul's imprint .She told me that we were creating our next lifetime when living this lifetime. She taught me something very important. She showed me reverence, self-love, respect, the honor of life, and one other thing, soul alignment. You can *untie the knots* when you apply soul alignment. This can take you very far with erasing karma or unfettering negative attachments, (fetters – anything that confines or restrains) The word "fetter" was originally applied specifically to a chain or shackle for the feet. This would stop you from moving forward or from walking your path and attaining soul growth. (See, *Unlimited Realities*)

Backstage, behind the curtain
Beyond our physical senses
The Universe moves and vibrates
With its hosts of Angel, Teachers, and Guides.

Holding within it magic and miracles
It's always here for you to reach for
Trust it as it orchestrates your life,
Unending and forever into eternity.

—EAJ 3/26/2020

Karma is action. For every action there must be a reaction or response, even if the response seems to be silence. It never really is silence, but a vibrating energy, hidden backstage until needed. Our present life karma key is held within our astrological chart at birth.

The universe is extremely precise. As Edgar Cayce taught, "The Law of Karma is exact." Because this is true on the planet Earth, then is must also be true beyond the physical plane as well. We pick our parents, our location of birth, pinpoint our karmic lessons in our birth chart and set up our primary family as well. The most important relationships we have are with the primary family. It is within this sphere that we experience other areas of life. When we can unfetter the karmic attachments within our primary, then we can begin to walk a path away from the shackles that bind us. Then the soul can grow and become one with itself, eventually expanding into the oneness of all.

Part of the karmic law is, "nothing happens by accident". Think about that for a moment. Dr. Deepak Chopra teaches us this principle as well as how to deal with the energies of attraction. It's all done within our mind and our thoughts. Thoughts are things. They carry an energy vibration, for good or for ill.

Karma works along with the Golden Rule; *do unto others what you'd want done unto you*. With Karma energy we can modify the rule to include all past lifetimes. What you have done in the past comes to you now, while what you are doing now is setting up your future life experiences.

Most of us know the saying, *"What goes around comes around"*. When you work with this energy, you can learn how to love, for learning how to love is learning how to die. Richard Bach once wrote, "Release it and let it go. If it come back to you, then you'll know it's real". Karma, as any of the higher vibration energies, teaches you love and responsibility. What is in your heart, what your intention is in every action, is what will come back to you. You can create "bad karma" or "good karma". It's your choice. There are no exceptions because Karma applies to every one equally. When you realize that Karma always takes care of any situation, then you can resolve sadness, hurt, or any negative feelings from your heart.

To heal your karma, seek out what lessons you need to learn and come to an inner agreement to be willing to learn them. Remember, they are contained within your astrological birth chart that you set up with your Divine teachers and guides before birth. The downside is to fail to learn from your mistakes, and many of us do. Of course, you'll have another chance by repeating this lifetime in your next life. That also shows up in your birth chart.

Louise Hay taught us to look into the mirror at your face, that beautiful face, and tell yourself you are bountiful, blissful, and beautiful. While looking, lock your eyes with the eyes in the mirror and think or say. "I love you." How does that make you feel? (It took me a few years to be able to do that simple act.)

Karma teaches us that we get exactly what we think we deserve. When I was learning about muscle testing, I asked my body how much money I would make this next year. I was shocked at the answer. It wasn't nearly enough to live on. I worked very hard on that subconscious belief. Basically my subconscious didn't think I deserved much, and I had to focus on my attitude because to transcend karma, you need to agree with your guides that you deserve more. You need to change the inner belief system by resolving your life's issues and allow more love into your life.

What's absolutely marvelous about all of this is that karma can be changed by uplifting your inner belief system. It can be transcended as you bring more love into your life, but first, you must allow your inner being to love who and what you are.

If the law of Karma is exact, then all karma comes up for payment over time, without exception. Whether is takes several lifetimes or just a few hours makes no difference. Always remember that your karma must be and will be brought into balance.

Healing Our Karma:

Forgiveness is surfacing in scientific studies as an important element in health and healing. The healing power of forgiveness has been scientifically documented. Forgiveness has been known to decrease physical pain and stress, strengthen the immune system, decrease the risk of heart attacks, strengthen relationships, and increase happiness and wholeness. Begin to forgive yourself and your heart will open up to begin to forgive others. This can remove feelings of prejudice and judgment and can come a long way to establish world peace.

FIVE things to forgive:

1. Forgive God for the separation from Him when you were created as an individual being. Relax, enjoy, and be in the highest energy and highest of spirits. Thank God and forgive. Remember always that your soul is always a part of the Divine and that you are never without God's influence, guidance, and protection.

2. Forgive your destiny and your karma. You didn't write your destiny, you earned it. You cannot do anything about it. You can simply live and resolve it, or not.

3. Forgive the environment, which is always challenging, and the cause and effect (daily karma) which is always happening. It isn't your life that matters, or what occurs, it's the courage and love you bring to each and every experience that counts. This builds Soul Character. (Remember one of my favorite sayings, *"The loving is easy, it's the living that's hard."* Frank Sinatra)

4. Forgive your capacity, or lack thereof, your ability, your duality. When asked, remember always that the Divine will come through for you.

5. Forgive yourself - and the fact that you have to go through all this. *("It's karma baby!"* Telly Sevalas)

All you have to remember is YOU. God rotates this Earth around our Solar System. He takes care of the birds, the flowers, the trees, the dolphins, etc. You can bet that He will always take care of you as well. It just may be time to raise your vibration and change your belief system. In God we trust. It is always God's world. We dwell in God's house. Just behave like a good guest. Be calm, be quiet, be restful, be humble, be harmonious, be with everything like

95

a human, and most of all, *Let It Be.*

Make yourself happy, make others happy and wear God's crown. Don't become spoiled or a clown. *"You are the highest of the incarnations on this planet. You are the crown success of God's kingdom."* (Yogi Bhajan)

Walk straight, walk tall and always stay in your truth. That's it! No left, no right. If you cannot keep the crown of the Divine on your own head, then you will live like a clown within your head. YOU decide. If you can practice these five points of self-forgiveness, you will find self-realization and increasing inner peace. You will find that the world is extremely friendly. You will uplift and change your karma, and create lot's of *good* karma.

If you don't, then my prayer is that you do not suffer much. My prayer is that the thirty-million God cells living within you, dancing within you, may protect you, and that your radiant body may always keep you radiant.

The fact is, God calls on you in every event and every experience you live. That's Karma. Answer the call. God has made you, so be it. God gives you your face, your figure, your facts along with Free Will. So - trust in God and keep going.

Here is a helpful Mantra Prayer to keep you in balance.

Song of the 144,000
from *The Immortal* - by J. J. Dewey

We thank you Father
That you have revealed to us
Your protective Universal Light;
That within this light is complete protection
From all destructive forces;
That the Holy Spirit permeates us
In this light, and wherever we will
The light to descend.

We thank you Father
That you fill us with your Love;
That within this Love is complete protection
From all destructive thoughts and feelings;
That the consciousness of Christ
Is lifted up in us in this Love,
And wherever we will the love to be enflamed.

We thank you Father
That You are in us, and we are in You;
That through us Your Will is sent forth
On wings of power;
That Your Purpose is accomplished on earth
As it is in heaven;
That through us, Your Light
And Love and Power
Is manifest to all
The Sons and Daughters of mankind.

Backstage
The Importance of Your Personal
Inner Connection

NOTES:

CHAPTER TWELVE

WHAT'S AHEAD FOR THE NEW DECADE

A Higher View — The Equality of Multi-dimensionality

These pages have reminded you that you are very magical. Let's take a little journey to share some of the beautiful things taking place that are also truly magical. There is nothing to fear by adapting this new concept Your whole spirit knows its way Home and this information is going to help you remember that, so take a breath with me for just a moment.

Breathe in

and as you release the breath, release all the tensions of the day. Let go of all those thoughts for just a moment. You can reclaim them on the other side of this journey if you wish, but for right now let us take you on a journey Twenty Years into the Future.

Twenty years from now, you will have a mix of energies and you will have the ability to experience it in a number of different ways. Why? Because there will be the possibility of more separation than you have on the planet even now. That separation will have a lot to do with basic ideals, such as where you see yourself, how you present yourself, and how well humans can change. Yes, many people have become set in their ways and defend their choices by never choosing again; minds are closed and unable to perceive a wider picture.

Twenty years from now, there will be ample opportunities for people to choose different paths and roads. There will be numerous ways of thinking and an array of abilities. So, you have some beautiful things on the horizon. You will be witnessing things lining up that you may not have seen coming. Understand, that some technologies and ideas have been dropped; done away with.

Many of your medical advances are ideas that have been channeled by medical experts. All the ideas are from the same place, for creativity comes from the same place, at different vibrationary levels. Many of you call it "channeling". Yes, the energy from *Universal Knowledge*, which is beyond the Astral Plane, is where the energy of absolute Truth lays. Now on planet Earth there are many beautiful channels lining up to bring you very valuable and important information and all of you are going to be using the information in the near future.

No More Secrets

Twenty years from now many forms of channeling will be honored and used in daily life. Yet, there will be those who try to misuse it for personal gain. You are seeing the rise in no more secrets, no more "fake" news. This is a natural evolution that is causing people to be more connected heart to heart. Humans are experiencing this as many secrets from the past are being uncovered.

Witness that sexual predators are no longer able to keep their actions hidden, as more and more people are speaking out. It is time. This is a natural evolution and leads to an era of *"No More Secrets on Earth."* As this energy progresses motivations of actions will be seen more clearly. Watch for the underhanded motivations; especially with the flow of money, as it has been a large contributor to the secrets that still are so prevalent. As secrecy continues to lessen, humans will begin to trust their hearts more than their heads, which opens the opportunity for more information to come down from the Universe.

Twenty years from now you will have several new and exciting technologies. Some of these have been put on Earth before, but could not take hold in one way or the other. Nikolai Tesla is one of the channels ready to bring in information, and there are many who can begin to hear this channel. Some may think these are their own 'ideas' but Spirit does not need to be recognized as long as the message comes forth for good use. When the receivers are ready, the information will be given freely.

One of the ideas that Tesla is dropping right now has been known as "free energy," which is the science of extracting energy from the ambient energy that is all around each one of you at this powerful time. This technology drop will first be seen in the areas of battery technology, but will quickly begin to evolve into larger discoveries.

There are also many channels opening that will work in harmony with the Earth in an entirely different way than you have been accustomed to before. This can greatly extend the timeline of planet Earth and help all of humanity evolve. Those of you with a spiritual awareness, who have worked with spirit more than technology, have some great movements coming as well. Spirit does not segment information into categories such as technology, medicine, or spirituality because it's a flowing energy. Categorizing is strictly a human action.

As new ideas arrive and technologies land through channels, it will cause a shift, and you will see a winding down of many things that are no longer needed. These new channel openings will cause great changes for all humans.

Twenty years from now there will be many who resist this change and wish to return to the good old days. Between now and then there will be more conspiracy theories surfacing than ever before. The way humans have received news has been eroded on Earth, which has caused a shift toward receiving news in untraditional ways.

Twenty years in the future humans will have found a way to resolve this mistrust by removing money from the equation. Just as today, there will still be many who hold tight to the idea of big conspiracies. Between now and then it will be become more evident that fear has been used to direct misinformation, and that will be the cause of much of the separation still seen on the Earth.

Mastery of Earth Harmony

There are certain cycles already in motion, which are no longer reversible at this point. Everything that can be mastered between now and then will not have to be experienced at the next level. You Lightworkers are simply changing form and that will become evident about twenty years from now. Ten years from now there will be no discussion nor argument about what you call "global warming," or the physical changes that are taking place on planet Earth.

It is not just about global warming; the ice age that will follow will be a huge change. This ice age begins in the present decade, the 2020's. Ten years from now very few people will dispute the timeline of the changing climate Earth. The hope is that this information will help everyone to start working more in harmony to reach a level of mastery with Spirit and the Earth.

Power ~ Harmony v.s. Force

The feminine energy will continue to rise on Earth over the next twenty years, at which time very few will doubt the equality of feminine energy. With a closer connection of all humans, a new form of power emerges. *Harmony will eventually take the place of force.* Of course, there will be throwbacks; people who still think they are in power in some way. They believe they must try to hold up the old ideals, so they will actively fight the changes until they are exhausted. Yes, change will be difficult for many. However, Spiritual advancement of humanity can create many opportunities to view things from a larger perspective.

Returning to Lightbody

Twenty years from now many of you will hold parts of your own Lightbodies and be able to work in them in conjunction with the physical body. This ability will open doors for many to see the possibilities and opportunities to create a new expression of humanity. It will bring hope to all who can recognize it changing. There will be less need for leaders and politicians, who will take on a new focus.

After several strong attempts at dictatorship the general public will see that game for what it is, then head it off before it can fully take form. Equality will once again become important.

As people start moving into their Lightbody there will be fewer illnesses; harmony with Earth will bring better health and longevity, as even a small portion of people begin to move into their Lightbody. This will not happen all at once but in increments, slowly increasing with just how much light your body can carry. That not only means bringing Light into the body, but also exuding Light and being able to reflect it in different ways. This is starting to happen to many of you even now in 2020.

When this first begins to happen, you will have a tendency to hold back your Light. You will see the effect it has on other people and you literally will try to hide it, which is a natural reaction of a human. However, twenty years from now you can all start walking more consciously in this Light because at that time it will be a common practice where people start moving in various stages of their Lightbodies. It can literally start to incarnate an entirely new dimension, and then you will start making up the new lifestyle and deciding how it will be played out.

Technologies and Spiritual Advancement

The technology is also advancing. This has been only a dream for many until now; colonization of Mars is one of these advancements. You will start to discover other places throughout the universe. Right away you begin to realize there are many more planets that could support life in some way. Working with the new technologies can help you to reach these areas and even live there.

But that is not the most important part, it is simply one of the exciting things that you will see as your technologies catch up with your spirituality. There will be a major spiritual awakening in the next twenty years and this spiritual movement will open the doors for technological advancements to grow. These two elements are connected. These new technologies have not been able to take root or grow because the vibration levels and spiritual advancement was not high enough to support it.

About twenty years from now (2038) your spiritual advancements will open the doors for some of your technologies. This will work in harmony with the Earth to help her in natural transitions. Does that mean that everyone will be on the same page at that point? No, it does not look that way at this point. Humans have a challenge: they support the decisions they make, no matter what evidence to the contrary is right in front of them. Humans are learning those lessons right now. The next few years will be turbulent and filled with these lessons. There will always be some who decide to stay behind and choose the old ways. We ask you not to judge them but to simply let them go in love.

Move forward in your own way, for you will be opening the doors for many. You have the ability to create a path further into the Universe, even into the next phase of life, which you are now starting to develop.

When you are in *unity consciousness*, after living your lifetime, you know you are part of everything. You feel everything and everyone; you are in balance naturally. It is quite exciting when you see it all from a higher perspective. Understand how much you are all alike, and how much you are part of everything. So, when you play this illusion of pretending to be separate you leave your memory, your spirit. Then your spirit incarnates into a body and you see yourself as a human, separate from each other. This is very exciting because it allows all of spirit, what you call God, to evolve and become self-aware in a physical body. Although seemingly you feel separate from the whole, when you are all connected you cannot see your *self*.

That is the one thing that God cannot do; God is not able to see its own reflection. So, here you are pretending to be separate and having an incarnation. When you were born you knew who you were, so you basically had to forget your true self, the Blessed Higher Self. You learned how to live in the illusion by pretending to be separate. Many actually learned how to do this from their parents; often learning what has been passed down generation to generation. You can see this playing out in your politics on Earth right now.

This is the new way of pretending to be a human, because now that the illusion is reaching a conclusion. You will be stepping into another lifetime or illusion. What is that one going to look like? Where is it going to be played?

What dimensional realities will be present? You cannot know that, because you have not yet decided the outcomes.

Twenty Years from Now

Yes, the magic has begun. Twenty years from now there will be a balance of density and Light. You have a choice as to where you wish to be, and twenty years from now is when you will start devising the new life.

You can start today by laying out potentials and dreaming. Take a look back at all the things that happened on this planet Earth over the last few million years where you have been doing all these lifetimes. You will start to develop new ideas, set conditions, and establish different boundaries so that you do not experience the same traps that you once did in the past.

Humanity will have new opportunities, and at some point you will start an entirely different lifetime. No, it does not have to begin with some little creature crawling out of the ocean, even though you may have done that yourself at some point. Instead, you will be able to create something very magical that can bring together many different places throughout the universe, which are playing these life games very similar to yours. You are already aware that you are not the most technically advanced of all the creatures throughout the universe. Yet humans have moved the dial further along than any. There are some that even know how to travel through time, using the orthogonal matrix.

The Future Is Bright – Wait Until You See What Is Coming!

Just be assured that the future is much brighter than you imagine. You need to remember that you have not done anything wrong. Wait until you see what is coming twenty years from now!

Magic and excitement will be in the air, along with many changes that will take place. Yes, there will also be the new technologies to help you make these transitions and to help balance the Earth. You will be able to master many things even before you start this new adventure

I can tell you that time is circular. You have a tendency to repeat things over and over again, even as you are playing this game of pretending to be human. You do not have to repeat the next life and that is an exciting possibility. Even though you may not know it, you hold many of the keys, which are very critical for this transition.

Nurture one another and play well together.

Ascension Clearing
Manage your new vibration energy

Learn to enter the *State of Being*, hold the new amber light, and work with the *two* heart centers to raise your vibration, and create and manifest your desires.

You can learn to be the creator of your reality – quickly – find something that's soft and feels good for you. Then soften yourself – to open and receive.

1) Discover your path and Soul gifts
2) Build up your inner power
3) Receive your New body and new story
4) Clear and strengthen your body vibration
5) Call on and work with your New 5th Dimension Guides
6) Learn to focus in the higher vibration to heal yourself, heal others, create, and merge with the Golden Light of the higher heart center.
7) Drop your resistances, drop the past

8) Allow your Power and Control to create a breakthrough
9) Learn to bring in and attract on that which you desire
10) Apply the New Spiritual Chakras
11) Work with the Magic of the Circle of Light – sending out energy to help others
12) Accomplishing Clarity is as good as it gets.

New Affirmation

I am satisfied where I am today, I am at peace – and open and eager to receive what's coming next.

CHAPTER THIRTEEN

BACKSTAGE HAS THE SOLUTION

Spiritual energy gives us a sense of belonging and the freedom to be spontaneous; to know we're supported by the invisible forces backstage in whatever we wish to do. It is a creative force that fills us with optimism, giving us the energy we need to achieve our dreams. Just pull out the props and use them as you will. It's a very subtle energy and yet it's incredibly powerful at the same time.

Anyone who is following their higher desires and creativity, who is being of genuine service to others, and who is coming closer to a realization of their own Divinity is invoking this energy, and it will always be there for you.
Energy healing is a form of alternative and complementary healing practices. It is a holistic approach believing that when the energy within the body becomes imbalanced, the result is illness. When you are spiritually developing, you, your essence, and your spiritual body are working together in the "flow", the bandwidth of the double helix energy that is now available. Spiritual (not religious) energy, vibrational radiance from all matter in all dimensions, including non-physical ones, is the emanation

of the clear, clean, loving, primordial energy that allows everything to exist. It's called the God-source, shakti, the chi or the energy of Love. Whatever name you give it doesn't matter. It's all the same, it's all one, and it's always present.

Call it into your world. Raise up your vibration, become whole and healed, and live life as you see fit with the center and balance of love, peace, and harmony.

In the meantime, here are some stories from two of my colleagues. People whom I greatly admire.

UNSEEN ENERGIES
BY **SHARON LYNN WYETH**

Unseen energy (the Backstage energy) is all around us. Even as it is unseen, it can be felt, similar to the wind created by a fan. We don't continue to see the blades turning as the fan becomes faster, yet we can definitely feel the result of the fan. The same is true of unseen energy. To that end, I would like to share some experiences where unseen energy was most significant.

My first experience knowing that unseen energy was real was when I was a senior in high school and invited to a tea party at my friend's house on a Saturday afternoon. I asked mom if I could use the car. She had replied that she wasn't planning on going anywhere, so yes. I no sooner had arrived at my friend's house, when I said, "My mom needs the car, I'll be back shortly." She was obviously confused as I had just arrived, and my mom hadn't called her house. How did I know that she needed the car? I didn't know how I knew; I just knew I had to go back home. Sure enough, my little sister had injured herself and needed to see our dad, who was a doctor, immediately. Mom dropped me back at the party on her way to my dad's office.

Today we would call what I experienced *telepathy*. Telepathy is a way of communicating with unseen energy. Over the years, there have been many times when I have received unsaid messages; from students in my classroom, to my own children. This caused my students to think I really understood them and enhanced my ability to answer their questions prior to the question even being asked. This occurred so often with my own children that they would get upset when I failed to receive their unspoken messages sent to me when they weren't home. They did not comprehend that if I was deeply concentrating on something else, then their message would not be received. They considered the telepathy between us as normal, not aware that it was my deep connection with them that allowed me to hear their message without the use of a phone. Telepathy utilizes unseen energies that are available to everyone; unseen but acknowledged by both parties involved.

It happened in the Denver, Colorado area. I had just shared my spiritual understandings and what I had received from Spirit with a large group at the home of my sponsor. A middle-aged man approached me at the end of the session and asked if I would come see his son. He informed me that his son was both blind, dumb, and disabled enough physically where he was restricted to a wheelchair, but he could understand sign language because he was taught it prior to losing his hearing. Would I come and have my team work with him?

111

Backstage
The Importance of Your Personal
Inner Connection

I had been the spiritual conduit, connecting with unseen energies, for the group that I call the *Light Keepers* for quite some time, and had been invited to numerous places to both speak on spiritual topics and to give personal readings. But this time it was different. This man was asking if I could come and help his child who needed assistance physically because his child was constantly in pain. I hesitated. I sensed that this wasn't my calling; I wished to facilitate others by sharing knowledge to correct or expand their thinking patterns. I didn't work with the physical body, or so I thought. Thus, I protested, saying my work was for more mental understanding, not for physical healings and suggested utilizing the services of chiropractors, massage therapists, and/or Rolfers, as they would be more helpful.

The Dad pleaded, reiterating his invitation, saying they had already tried alternative therapies, and would I please just come and try? My sponsor answered for me, committing me to appear the following day. I reluctantly went. I said my usual prayer after introductions were made. The dad was there to communicate for his son and sat near him to facilitate that communication. I sat across the room from the child being totally uncomfortable with what I was requested to do.

My Light Keeper team was asked if they could please relieve the man's son from his physical pain. I allowed my team the use of my body, instead of just my brain, such that my hands flew through the air doing who knows what. My eyes stay closed when I am hearing Spirit so that I am not distracted and can more easily solely focus on what Spirit is conveying.

It wasn't long before the son started making grunting sounds, and began communicating with his dad. He was asking that my team slow down the process as the energy he felt was coming onto him too strongly! What a

112

shock! Here was a blind child, who could not see what we were doing, could *know* exactly when energy was being transferred to him, and when it wasn't! He wasn't complaining when the energy was slow, yet repeatedly asked for the energy to slow down anytime my team sped it up.

I was amazed by this child's perceptions. The father thanked us profusely when we left and his son was out of pain. The unseen forces had been at work and it was successful! It also frightened me; it was so obvious that something was transpiring between my spiritual team and this child. As I look back, there was nothing to be afraid of for me; yet I was. I was afraid of being expected to pull through that type of energy again!

Yet, after that experience, the unseen forces continued to be active in my life in various ways. For example, I had recently finished reading Marlo Morgan's book, *Messages Down Under,* when I fell down the steps leaving my dad's place. He had already closed the door and said goodbye. I couldn't get up. My left foot was so damaged that you could see the broken bones doing their best to poke through the foot's skin. I was in agony and considered crawling on my hands and knees back up to dad's door to get help or I could experiment with a method of healing explained in Morgan's book. A kind couple approached me before I could decide what to do. They had seen me fall and came over to help me get up. Together they helped me limp to my car. Grateful that I was driving an automatic, I decided to drive to my sister's where the family would be gathering that evening for dinner.

I got help getting out of the car by numerous nephews and nieces who were playing outside, and deposited myself on a dining room chair so that I could keep my oldest sister company while she was busy preparing the meal. I asked if she would be willing to help me with my foot. I knew where our hands needed to go and what to say, but with my foot in this much agony, and the angle that I would need to be when using my hands, it wasn't going to be possible for me to perform this process without help.

So, I asked my sister if she would assist and told her exactly where to place her hands. I let her know if she could just hold that position until I was done thinking what had to be thought, (the telepathic healing message to my body) it would be greatly appreciated. My sister laid her hands crosswise on my foot, avoiding the area where the bone was pushing the skin up in the air making my foot look like a flagpole. I focused on the thoughts I remembered of what Morgan explained in her book. Then I remained sitting in the chair, and waited until my dad arrived for dinner.

I asked Dad to examine my foot when he entered the kitchen. He came over, examined it, feeling it all around before stating, "You are lucky, nothing is broken. You just bruised it." My sister who was carrying a large pot full of boiling water and cooked spaghetti noodles from the stove to the sink, almost dropped the pan. She had seen my bone poking up under my skin and was sure my dad's diagnosis was wrong.

However, when she came back to look at my foot, she was shocked. The bone had repositioned itself correctly and was no longer looking like a flagpole! Sure enough, I was able to move like nothing had happened. Except something had happened and it had been plenty more than a little bruising. Today, I feel I had that experience just to know that Morgan's methodology that she learned from the Aborigines, actually works. I have since used this method successfully on others.

Lastly I'd like to share unseen energies at work that still baffle me on how the universe pulled this one off. I was invited to come talk and give readings in Marin County north of San Francisco. My sponsor had sent me directions on which bus to catch from the airport, where to get off of the bus, and then to call her on the pay phone at that location. I would be a few blocks from her home. She would be able to drive down to get me without waking her two small children because the parking lot was so close to her house, and it would be late at night.

I followed the directions well, easily finding the bus from the San Francisco airport to Marin County. The place where I got off the bus was dark and totally deserted, without any streetlights. This place was a little more than a round driveway with a phone booth. I went to the phone booth to make the call. That is when I panicked. I did not have any change in my wallet, so I could not call my sponsor! Here I was, in an area totally unknown to me, not knowing the sponsor's address, just her phone number. I had no idea which way to go to even walk to her house, there was no one around, and it was pitch black outside. I panicked and immediately asked the universe for help.

I no sooner requested help than a man taped my shoulder from behind. He asked me if I needed change. I said yes, and asked if he had any extra change. The man stated that he had three quarters on him. I gleefully traded his three quarters for my dollar bill. With inner gratitude I inwardly thanked Spirit because I realized that I was saved. I immediately turned around to put a quarter in the phone and when I reeled back around to thank the man for his kindness, there was no one there. Imagine how quickly you can turn around and then swing right back to your starting place. You can do this in seconds, as I did. The man was gone! There were no vehicles around, and no people near me, not even anywhere on the street. A person had manifested himself to provide quarters to me and then disappeared!

Needless to say the rest of my time at this event went smoothly, and I always have money and an address when I travel now. Even though this happened many years ago, years before cell phones, I still cannot tell you where that man came from, nor where he went so quickly, However, I remain grateful to this day.

There are unseen energies occurring around us all of the time. Sometimes it's blatantly obvious, like in that dark parking lot in Marin County, and sometimes it's obscure. Yet, there is never a time when the energies stop. They are simply waiting for a signal from you and directions about what is needed.

FRANK ST. JAMES

Back in the early 1970's I was living in Massachusetts. I got a call from a woman, Ruth, who wanted to host a psychic party at her farm, The Van, which I understood was built in 1680. I felt the ancient energy coming from it right away.

I was feeling some interesting energies on the day I wanted to know the names of the people who were at the party. When I opened the door and walked in, there was a *spirit* leaning against a beehive oven. This was a huge beehive oven used back in that timeframe. I described the entity to the owner and she said that it was the previous owner who they had bought the property from. He seemed to be in a pretty good mood so I didn't banish him.

We all went up to the second floor and to a room that nobody's been never been able to sleep in. The room was always cold, no matter what the temp was outside. This was where we set up a card table in front of the fireplace and I began to give my readings.

Towards the end of my last reading, with Ruth, the present owner, the door shut across from me. I had been taping all the readings so everybody got their reading on tape. As I began talking to Ruth, I said,
"I know this room was never really refinished."

The room still had the wide floorboards and the atmosphere in there was kind of electrical. As I started to talk to her I said,
"I sense there's an ounce of gold beneath us under the floorboards."

As we continued to do the reading, in my left eye I saw a baby in a crib being rocked. The baby looked up at me and started crying. Telepathically I started to work with the baby and I calmed her down, gave her some healing energy, and told her to go to her mother. Suddenly her mother gathered the baby up into her arms. I sensed that her mother had been waiting over 300 years to do that simple act. Then the scene disappeared!

I told Ruth about it but she didn't hear the crying. I finished my readings and then I left.

Two weeks later, Ruth gave me a call and said that when she played the tape back she heard the baby crying on the tape. Also that particular night they had a lot of people that stayed over. They used that room, and nobody had a problem sleeping there.

I found that I had been able to clear the room of the negative energies and learned that it was an energetic porthole to the other side – in the past.

The family began to renovate it as an extra bedroom, and when they tore up one of the floorboards in front of the fireplace, they found a gold tooth.

Backstage
The Importance of Your Personal
Inner Connection

"There's your ounce of gold , Frank," Ruth said laughing. After that happened, I managed to get a duplicate tape of her reading with me.

I had been working with a small group of professors and scientists know as the Egypt Club. I gave past life regressions back to Egypt and everybody regressed back to various time periods, to find out what kind of a past life they may have had there.

There was a scientist, Barbara, who was working with sound. Barbara and I talked about what I had on tape from the farm, so she invited me over to her home in Cambridge where she had her lab. She worked with a laser beam and sound.

We started to play the tape and you could hear Ruth and I talking. The laser beam from her scientific equipment kept throwing up a pattern on the screen as the sound waves or our voices hit the equipment. When it came to the sound of the baby crying, it just went silent. It did not register any type of sound waves. We were both amazed. There was nothing like this back in the early 1970's, living in Massachusetts

In the spring of 1995, I was reading for a girl, Maria, in my home. She was going back to Columbia, and had already purchased her ticket. She was flying from Newark Airport in New Jersey to Miami, changing planes, and then going on to Columbia. I started to work with the energies and did not feel good about the second flight. I advised her to take a different flight from Miami to Columbia.

When she got to the Miami airport, she was on line for the original flight, but became very nauseous. Figuring this was some kind of an energetic signal, she changed her ticket to a later flight.

The original flight never made it to Columbia. It crashed into the side of a mountain on its approach, and all were lost.

Strangely enough, in the year 2000, another young lady, Lori, came for a reading. She was concerned about who would be walking her dog. I asked her what happened to her father.

She said he was a pilot. She explained that when he was piloting the plane going to Columbia, it hit the side of a mountain and all on board were killed. I knew instantly that it was his plane that went down in 1995, when Maria had changed her flight to save her life.

I feel that's another example of going into different dimensions, but to actually have it come back to me and finish up within my vision was quite extraordinary.

I have told some stories of how Backstage works. There are many, many more. If you have any you would like to share, please let me know. They will be posted on my Backstage page at new-visions.com.

Backstage
The Importance of Your Personal
Inner Connection

NOTES:

Elizabeth Joyce

CHAPTER FOURTEEN

EXCERCISES TO REACH THE PROPS
BACKSTAGE

Your Soul is a dynamic, growing body of energy, which is responsive to your needs and develops, clears, and grows in proportion to the energy, meditation, and attention you give it.

It is impressive to consider the unlimited potential, infinite possibilities, and unlimited realities we each possess and the extraordinary opportunities that are presented to us each day. Yet we rarely use these opportunities and often even fail to recognize the relevance of life's experiences and the possibility of achieving our life desires.

Let's work on how we can create greater clarity in our lives by getting out of our own way. Let's allow the powerful forces of the Universe and Truth to govern our lives to help us learn and create our most productive life experiences.

It isn't bad luck or an insensitive Universe that deals you "blows" and obstacles. Rather, it is your own inner motivations, attitudes, and personal beliefs that powerfully influence your life, drawing to you what you

121

expect to receive, and actually may visualize inwardly through your fears. You will receive that which you feel you deserve and that for which you will settle.

Your vulnerabilities and weaknesses become the arenas for optimal change and growth. Problems bring opportunities and Soul growth, depending on how you solve them. Whether a physical disease, financial or family concerns, a deteriorating relationship, or unhappiness and dissatisfaction with your job is the issue, the area where you most need to direct your full attention is the one that you would most like to avoid.

While it is natural to avoid the pain of looking into your life and seeing where it doesn't work, this pattern of looking the other way becomes a self-perpetuating excuse to avoid changing what is the source of the pain. It is called *denial* and is the root of fear. Soul growth begins the willingness to consider your life from a different vantage point, including new perceptions about your life in relation to other people, and in relation to a higher intelligence, which makes room for the fulfillment you most want. This opening brings a chance for the Universe to step in and do its thing – bringing about what you most need to fulfill your desires and step upwards in body, mind and spirit.

When you feel empowered and in control of your life, when things are going smoothly for you, the natural tendency is to coast. When the bottom falls out, when things go wrong, you then pay attention to yourself, your dreams, your fears, and your needs in a very different way. You have nothing to lose by allowing the walls, blocks, fears and obstacles in your life fall away. The fear is is usually of the unknown. The hesitancy is to be different from what you have learned and to take a chance on a new way of expression.

As you learn to look at your life honestly, increasing your self-awareness, without excuses and defenses, and preconceived conditions, you will find the levels of fears and anxiety diminish. The willingness to re-evaluate the current you and the possibility of creating, with care and understanding, a new you, is what turns limitation into opportunity, destructive old patterning into viable, healthy new pathways for growth and success. Remember, every day you live in this lifetime, along with every decision you make and every interaction you share – you are setting up your karma for your next lifetime.

The natural fears of loss, abandonment, death and failure exist just under the surface in our daily living and are triggered by experiences that show us all too clearly our own mortality. These fears can have the effect of causing us to think long and hard about the significance of our life, its meaning and its value. Feeling that we have a purpose and are of value in life is our single most critical need. However, it is very easy in the hurriedness of our lives, to only consider the world in front of us and not look at the entire picture of responses and events.

We make mistakes with others and ourselves when we work with EGO, fear, and the *me only* attitude. Since we all actually exist in a greater dimension of life and have the potential of accessing a greater relationship to an expanded Universe, then it becomes our choice to set the intention as to when we want to begin that journey. We can keep the blinders on and think that life "happens" to us, or we can wake up and begin to understand these energies and learn how to work within and with them to enhance our lives and our future. We either begin this now, in this lifetime, or stay at our birth vibration level and begin again, in another.

When sorting through these opportunities for change and growth, you will find the process painful. We all have thin veneers of self-assurance and wellbeing surrounding us, which cause us to think that our life is under control. When we begin to open to Spirit and realize that the struggle to find meaning, health, and happiness is everyone's struggle, then we feel less self-conscious about our difficulties and settle down to a serious and sincere search for the value and meaning of our own lives.

The Master said, *"If you do good to even one of my children, you are doing good to me."* If you can save one life during your life span, you have achieved something. To choose to help with many lives through kindness and healing work is Service of the Soul and the Universe.

It is important to have a clear picture of what your current beliefs are about the Universe and your life in relation to this Universe.

Following are some exercises to help you canter, clear, and focus.

Exercise One – Emotional Alignment
Purpose: Mood matching
To better understand your spouse, friends, or co-workers in an effort to create peaceful conditions in your lives.

Pair up and sit face to face with your partner.
Take turns *scanning* each other's energy telepathically, looking for emotional vibrations. The person being scanned sits quietly with eyes closed, and projects energy toward scanner. The scanner has eyes open and may use telepathy, and aura reading abilities to come up with conclusions. Do not comment in return – just listen and allow your body to absorb what you've learned. Wait 24 hours; meditate on their message, then discuss.

Share your results, and thank your partner for his/her insights

Exercise Two – Mental Telepathy
Purpose: Experience the Oneness vibration
To detect the power of your connection to each other.

Pair up and sit face to face with your partner.
Take turns sending a number between 1 and 5 to the other's Third Eye. The sender and the receiver both have their eyes fixed on each other's Brow Chakra or Third Eye.

Share your results, and see how close you are to achieving Oneness by direct telepathy. (detecting the correct number, or coming close to it).
Now surround your team in protective white light. Perceive the unit of One that you have created, and try the exercise again. How do your results differ from before the addition of White Light and higher energies were added?

Exercise Three — 8th Chakra Meditation
Purpose: To open and spin the Eighth Chakra

Best to play ARDAS or peaceful meditation music.

Sit in a chair with both feet flat on the ground, legs uncrossed. Make sure your spine is straight. Close your eyes and visualize yourself standing amidst the most Rainbow-like beautiful energy. Visualize yourself standing in a beautiful amber-golden mist.

Take a deep breath.

It is important to feel very comfortable within this golden energy that takes on the shape of your energy field, beginning to rise up and connect you to your Spiritual Chakras.

Take another deep breath.

See within your mind's eye your Blessed Higher Self – your *Universal Body Self,* contained within the four levels of your Aura, and with that vision— claim yourself to be a powerful being by repeating the *Ascension Invocation for the 8th and 9th Chakras within your mind.*

Claim yourself as a powerful healer, creator, and co-creator of this world, working alongside the **One that Creates All**, joining together and co-creating your life, your miracles, and your preferred existence here on Earth.

Take a deep breath.

Activate this beautiful amber/golden energy that you are enveloped in as you draw within the power and the strength to practice your intention by moving yourself into a new power of thought by allowing the Divine Will of the Supreme God Light to be integrated into your entire Universal Being.

Take a deep breath.

Now imagine a most beautiful silver energy manifesting on the inside of the amber/golden energy, insulating the three original levels of your Aura, while providing your amber/golden shield with a liquid silver energy.

Take a deep breath.

Remind yourself that you are an expression of fluid love as you become the flow of unconditional love towards the Self and all others. Remind yourself of the feminine aspect of the Universal Body that always supports you in the highest and best way for you to remain flexible, and in so doing, embrace *the Fifth Dimension harmonies*, the flexible side of your personality, by allowing the Creative God Light to create within you the energetic vibration that is needed for you to transform your life.

Take a deep breath.

Now connect your heart center energy to the silver and amber/golden energies. If you need to place your hand on your heart to connect to the reality of your pulsating heart do so, once again connect to the pulse of your heart. Connect your heart energy to the heart of your etheric plasma, the Universal Body, thus connecting your beating heart to the amber/gold and silver lining around your aura, attached to the 9th Chakra at the back of your neck, where the brain joins the spine. You do this by sending unconditional love into this area —the part of your physical reality forming your etheric outline—therefore with every beat of your heart send unconditional love into the spaces that exist between the spaces that surround you.

Fill your auric field with this amber/gold and silver light. Send this light of love vibration to fill up all of the particles of light that exists between your physical and non-and-physical localities.

Take a deep breath.

Visualize your entire energy field filling up with Light and love as you visualize your entire energy field also filling with soft pink and amber/gold on the outside of your energy field, and silver on the inside edge (the fourth level of your aura) of your energy field. Allow the pink Love energy to fill up your energy field as it carries this light frequency and sound of unconditional love. Allow it to infiltrate your etheric—Universal anatomy, as you float within the most exquisite and most beautiful plasma of etheric unconditional love.

Now—begin to visualize that the amber/golden energy that encapsulates the outside of your energy field sending triggers of energy toward your inner heart pulse (4th Chakra), an energy that creates a sonic vibration of sacred sound and light as it births two golden spheres of energy that float from the 9th Chakra and come to lodge themselves within your Heart and Root Chakra. The amber/golden vibration of your Universal Light Body gives of itself, creating a new golden energy star template lodged within your Heart and Root Chakras.

Take a deep breath.

You are now connecting with every Angelic and Archangelic energy known and unknown to you at the level of your Heart and Root Chakras.

Please understand that the time has come for you to *let go of the control you have over others by allowing them to let go of the control they have over you.*

Begin to live through your heart, and make a point of shining your light towards others no matter their response. Connect to the *love crystals at the Heart Center*, allowing these energies to transform all of the energy that prevents you from claiming your magnificence as an Angelic Fifth Dimensional Human.

Allow all the blame and judgment that is so easily passed on to you even by those close to you, to wash over you, to slide away from you and set the intent at this level of your awareness to have absolutely all negativity transmuted by the Angels of Light.

Now—release this amber/golden orb of energy from the Root allowing it to travel upwards through your Crown Chakra lodging itself into your 8th Chakra.

Take a deep breath.

At this level, is there anything that you can think of while dwelling within this energy that makes you feel uncomfortable? Now is the time to take note of and work with it. It is a misplaced filament.

Take a deep breath.

Allow this angelic amber/golden orb to ascend—lodging itself within your solar plexus. Using this energy at this level to help you make friends with all of the aspects of the Universal self you still feel incongruent with.

Allow this energy to bring into balance all that is needed for you to practice unconditional love by loving the lower and higher Self completely.

Take a deep breath.

Allow this orb of amber/golden light to travel up through the Heart Chakra, pulsating, lodging within the 10th Chakra—the high heart center just above the 8th Chakra.

This is your Sacred Heart Center.
Make a commitment this day to do all you humanly can to spread love and enlightenment out into the world, to others. One of the easiest ways of doing this is to connect frequently with the energy of the Heart Center Love Crystals.

Take a deep breath.

Now allow this energy to ascend slowly from the Lower Heart Center — clearing as it transcends the Throat Center, piercing through to the Third Eye center, through the Crown Center, through the Pyramid of the 8th Chakra, through the Star Triad of the 9th Chakra, and lodges itself resting at the top of the 10th Chakra. Floating just above the 8th Chakra you now have an amber/golden etheric orb of Light which will allow you to work at this particular stage with all that is needed for you to integrate the Spiritual Chakras up to this point and realize the truth of your Angelic/Universal self.

Take a deep breath.

Now bring your attention to the inner silver energy that insulates your etheric membrane, at the fourth-third level of you Aura, as this energy also gives of itself, creating a most beautiful protection and fluidity that manifests as a silver bubble right in the very core of the golden orb.

Backstage
The Importance of Your Personal
Inner Connection

Take a deep breath.

The golden orb is about 2.5cm in thickness and about 9cm in diameter and floating within its core is a silver bubble of energy small enough to fit into the orb core. Now, gently lower this orb or light until it fits into the top triangle of the 9th Chakra—at the point of the 8 1/2 Chakra. In other words, allow the lower edge of the orb to come to rest on the flat end of the downward pointing triangle that forms part of the star-triad energy within the 9th chakra. In time this will form a support for many other orb energies from the higher chakras, to be birthed within your physical being.

Take a deep breath.

Now visualize within the very core of the silver energy contained within the amber/golden matrix a mother-of-pearl flame about 2.5cm in height, of an iridescent mother-of-pearl vibration.

You have the **platinum flame** within the iridescent *'mother-of-pearl-like'* vibration at the center of the 9th Chakra and now you have the iridescent *mother-of-pearl flame* within the silver/amber/gold or *relating platinum energy* of the 10th chakra. (The new Heart Center) You are connected to the vibrations and Light of the 10th Chakra, and the activation will begin at its own rate in its own way, naturally.

Know that this is only the beginning stage of activating the powerful energy of the Spiritual Chakras within your physical energy field. Few will accept this energy well. Others will find it to be a bit intense; either way simply relax into it. If you feel uncomfortable drink some water and feel yourself letting go and merging into it.

Take a deep breath.

Relate to these powerful vibrations emitted from the golden sphere and see how the gold and silver along with the mother-of-pearl energies pulsates light frequencies into the rest of your chakras.

First of all begin to visualize these energy orbs of light being transmitted from the 10th Chakra into the 9th, then 8th, then 7th, and so forth all the way down into the Root Center Take your time.

Now visualize how the mother of pearl energy increases in vibration now that the amber/golden and silver energies have laid the foundation for this powerful activation by sparking activity within your auric membranes. Allow the mother-of-pearl energy being emitted by the flame of this center to increase in vibration until your entire energy field vibrates on the frequency of mother-of-pearl.

Now within this powerful transformation of your energy field—claim your authentic angelic Universal Self at one with your human angel. Claim yourself as a Universal light worker, a planetary grid keeper, a divine magical-mystical being that lives in miracles, creates in miracles, and expresses only that which is of the most powerful unconditional love.

In so doing claim yourself as a being who chooses to do, to say, to think and share only that which uplifts others and to do so by practicing forgiveness of the self, claiming yourself as a most powerful being that trusts your Spiritual Ego to guide you instead of allowing the lower ego to take you off guard. Claim yourself as a wonderful emotional being, a sexual being, an earth being that claims the creative orb that is alive within you. With that, also remember that as a creative being, a multi-dimensional being, no matter the differences between you and your family and friends, what matters is for you to continue giving your God-Spark Light to bless them. Allow this your closed eyes—and see the *Divine Universal Light* moving within you.

Take a deep breath. OPEN your eyes.

Ground yourself–properly anchoring your energy though your Zero Chakras at the balls of the feet into the earth, making sure you are thoroughly grounded. Take three deep breaths. If you feel a swirling or are a bit dizzy, stay put, open your eyes and reach upward with your arms.

Before leaving, make sure that you are fully back into this NOW space.

Exercise Four—Setting an Intention
Experiencing the fullness of choice is the fuel upon which the soul develops. Choices continually bring to the conscious mind the opportunity to re-evaluate past decisions in light of a wider understanding of life and your purpose. Considering choices provides the opportunity for your next moment of life to exist at a deeper level of intuitive understanding, one that will reflect the greater wholeness of the Universe.

You cannot make a wrong choice within the power of Universal Law *because the reason for your choices is to expand the usable energy of the soul.*

Developing your inner *Sanctuary* is the key to expanding this energy on all multi-levels of the body/mind/spirit in a combination form. This means that the available energy for your use in pursuing your spiritual goals is increased when you pay attention to the choices in your life. The greater your willingness to accept the challenges of making those choices, the greater the degree of your Soul Energy and thus the greater degree of the spiritual life force energy that will flow within your body.

The fuel of the soul, the meditative Fifth Dimension energies, exists as a force of change, and if you make certain choices after meditation and tune in to the direction of your Blessed Higher Self, certain consequences follow. Yet this energy – this force beyond us yet within us – guides us in choosing to experience life in all of its differences, flavors and dimensions, which adds perspective and direction to the ultimate path of learning and purpose for each life time. In other words, the courage to consider choices, and to follow through with your inner decisions, along with the change that inevitably follows, is the power of the life experience and certainly fuels the development of the soul.

Consider this: *Your Soul is a dynamic, growing body of energy, which is responsive to your needs, and develops, clears and grows in proportion to the energy, meditation and attention you give it.*

It is impressive to consider the unlimited potential, infinite possibilities, and unlimited realities we each possess and the extraordinary opportunities that are presented to us each day. Yet we rarely use these opportunities and often even fail to recognize life's experiences and the possibility of achieving our life desires.

Let's work on how we can create greater clarity in our lives by getting out of our own way. Let's allow the powerful forces of the Universe and Truth govern our lives to help us learn and create our most productive life experiences.

It isn't bad luck or an insensitive Universe that deals you "blows" and obstacles. Rather, it is your own inner motivations, attitudes, and personal beliefs that powerfully influence your life, drawing to you what you expect to receive, and actually may visualize inwardly through your fears. You will receive that which you feel you deserve and that for which you will settle. Your vulnerabilities and weaknesses become the arenas for optimal change and growth. Problems bring opportunities and Soul growth, depending on how you solve them.

Whether a physical disease, financial or family concerns, a deteriorating relationship or unhappiness and dissatisfaction with your job is the issue, the area where you most need to direct your full attention is the one that you would most like to avoid. While it is natural to avoid the pain of looking into your life and seeing where it doesn't work, this pattern of looking the other way becomes a self-perpetuating excuse to avoid changing what is the source of the pain. It is called denial and is the root of fear. Soul growth begins the willingness to consider your life from a different vantage point, including new perceptions about your life in relation to other people, and in relation to a higher intelligence, which makes room for the fulfillment you most want.

This opening brings a chance for the Universe to step in and do its thing – bringing about what you most need to fulfill your desires and step upwards in body, mind and spirit.

When you feel empowered and in control of your life, when things are going smoothly for you, the natural tendency is to coast. When the bottom falls out, when things go wrong, you then pay attention to yourself, your dreams, your fears, and your needs in a very different way. You have nothing to lose by allowing the walls, blocks, fears and obstacles in your life fall away. The fear is the unknown. The hesitancy is to be different from what you have learned and to take a chance on a new way of expression. As you learn to look at your life honestly, increasing your self-awareness, without excuses and defenses, preconceived conditions, you will find the levels of fears and anxiety diminish.

The willingness to re-evaluate the current you and the possibility of creating, with care and understanding, a new you, is what turns limitation into opportunity, destructive old patterning into viable, healthy new pathways for growth and success. Remember every day you live in this lifetime, along with every decision you make and every interaction you share – you are setting up your karma for your next lifetime.

The natural fears of loss, abandonment, death and failure exist just under the surface in our daily living and are triggered by experiences that show us all too clearly our own mortality. These fears can have the effect of causing us to think long and hard about the significance of our life, its meaning and its value. Feeling that we have a purpose and are of value in life is our single most critical need. However, it is very easy in the hurriedness of our lives to only consider the world in front of us and not look at the entire picture of responses and events.

We make mistakes with others and ourselves when we work with EGO, fear, and the *me only* attitude. Since we all actually exist in a greater dimension of life and have the potential of accessing a greater relationship to an expanded Universe, then it becomes our choice to set the intention as to when we want to begin that journey. We can keep the blinders on and think that life "happens" to us, or we can wake up and begin to understand these energies and learn how to work within and with them to enhance our lives and our future.
We either begin this now, in this lifetime, or stay at our birth vibration level and begin again, in another.

When sorting through these opportunities for change and growth, you will find the process painful. We all have thin veneers of self-assurance and wellbeing surrounding us, which cause us to think that our life is under control. When we begin to open to Spirit and realize that the struggle to find meaning, health and happiness is everyone's struggle, then we feel less self conscious about our difficulties and settle down to a serious and sincere searching for the value and meaning of our own lives.

The Master said, *"If you do good to even one of my children, you are doing good to me."*

If you can save one life during your life span, you have achieved something. To choose to help with many lives through kindness and healing work is Service of the Soul and the Universe.

It is important to have a clear picture of what your current beliefs are about the Universe and your life in relation to this Universe.

Exercise Five— Writing the Forgiveness letter

Sometimes it is truly hard to forgive, or understand why someone is so upset with you that you are asking their forgiveness. You cannot fake forgiveness. You cannot say, "I forgive you", with any force or power unless it is truly felt in the heart.

Many times it's our primary family where forgiveness is sought. As has been explained to you before, these are the most important relationships because they are always karmic. Although you can forgive others, you can never make anyone forgive you; you can only ask for it. There are always two sides.

However, you can forgive even the most difficult of upsets in a relationship. You must not expect forgiveness in return, but wipe your heart clean of the disturbance. This act takes courage and surrender.

If the other person is reluctant to forgive you, there is one thing you can do that will not intrude on their Free Will decision, not to forgive.

This exercise must be done with an open heart. You are sending out the energy of love, honor, respect, and acknowledgement of their Soul.

You will need a pen and paper. This exercise cannot be done on a computer email or in a text. It must be hand written, in order to provide the proper energy necessary.

Dear person to forgive, (write their name)

I am truly sorry that I ever hurt you and I ask that you forgive me for everything I've done and everything I haven't done, past, present, and future.

As I forgive you for everything you've done and everything you haven't done, past, present and future.

That's it! No more, no less. No rehashing, no apologies, nothing. Just that *Soul Statement* is all that is necessary. Then mail the letter to the person you are forgiving or to the person you want to forgive you.

This is a very powerful exercise and works as long as you have peace and love in your heart.

The CoronaVirus

By breaking the Natural Law of Rhythm, man has disorganized the forces which, rightly used, tend to bring the body into a sound and healthy condition. By so doing, he has laid the foundation for that general debility the Corona Virus and those inherent organic tendencies which predispose a man to ill health and which permit entrance into the system of those germs and bacteria which produce the outer forms of a serious disease.

When humanity regains an understanding of the right use of time (which determines the Law of Rhythm on the physical plane), and can determine the proper cycles for the various manifestations of the life force upon the physical plane, then what was earlier an instinctual habit will become the intelligent usage of the future.

This information will constitute an entirely new science. The rhythm of the natural processes while the establishing, as habits, the correct cycles of physical functioning, will bring about a new era of health and of sound physical conditions for the entire race. The word "establishing" is used as the focus of radical attention shifts into the region of the higher values, where the physical vehicle will gain enormously; good health - through right rhythmic living, plus correct thinking and Soul contact - will then become permanently established

Exercise to help prevent the virus, and help with allergies as well as the common cold.

You will need a teakettle to boil water, a glass dish or pot to hold the steaming hot water and a towel and Vicks Vapro Rub.

Boil the water in the teakettle and pour it into the glass bowl. Apply the Vicks to each nostril of your nose. Put the towel over your head to make a tent effect. Bend over the hot water with the towel over your head and the front of the towel covering the bowl of steaming water. Allow the steam to flow up through your nostrils.

Take a deep breath.

Hold the steam inside your naval passage.

Count to 16 and release the breath.
Do this 16 times.

The virus cannot live in heat, so this exercise should kill any germs present. It's also a great way to clear congestion from allergies or a cold.

HEALTHY TIPS:

Avoiding close contact with sick individuals, frequently washing your hands with soap and water, not touching the eyes, nose, or mouth with unwashed hands, wearing disposable gloves when out shopping, especially when opening steel doors or using shopping carts, wearing a protective breathing mask, and practicing good respiratory hygiene. Also drinking my herbal Health and Healing Elixir Tea and clearing your space with my Brite-Clearing Formula Spray will be helpful.

Backstage
The Importance of Your Personal
Inner Connection

NOTES:

BOOK LIST

You Own The Power - Rosemary Altea

Hands of Light - Barbara Brennan
Light Emerging - Barbara Brennan

*The Seven Laws Of Success—Dr. Deepak Chopra

*The Immortal—JJ Dewey

Eternal Words—JJ Dewey

*Under An Ionized Sky—Elana Freeland

Living In The Light—Shakti Gwain

Initiation—Elisabeth Haisch

The Power of Force - David Hawkins

*You Can Heal Your Life - Louise Hay

The Energy Codes—Lee Harris

The New Spiritual Chakras — Elizabeth Joyce

*The Remnant - Mary La Croix

*MF—D 5G ———— Dr. Joseph Mercola

The Energy Codes—Dr. Sue Morter

**The Untethered Soul — Michael A. Singer

*The Timeless Path - Swami Ramakrishananda Puri

*The Third Eye - T. Lobsang Rampa

Man's Eternal Quest - Parmahansa Yogananda

* = Highly Recommended

ABOUT THE AUTHOR

Elizabeth Joyce

Born as one of two sets of identical twins, Elizabeth Joyce has been psychic since birth. Named one of the *World's Greatest Psychics* (Citadel Press, 2004), she is profiled in twelve books. She is a spiritual healer and gives personal psychic readings worldwide. Ms. Joyce is a professional Astrologer, Spiritual Counselor, Energy Healer, Clairvoyant Messenger, and teaches the new energies of the Fifth Dimension.

Elizabeth has been a writer and columnist for thirty years, has authored nine books, and is currently writing Astrology columns for *Wisdom Magazine, and OMTimes Media*. Her articles have appeared in *Planetary Wedding, the Enquirer, Natural Awakenings, The Sedona Journal of Emergence, Wisdom Magazine,* the *New York Daily News* and the *New York Times*. Elizabeth has been teaching metaphysical classes for the past thirty years. In 1986, just before the Harmonic Convergence, she was blessed to be initiated into the Hopi Tribe by Grandfather. She was named one of the *Top 100 Psychics in America* in 2014 and is a frequent guest on *Coast to Coast AM* with George Noory.

Elizabeth has studied with Margaret Stettner, Indira Ivey, Louise Hay, Dr. Deepak Chopra, Yogi Bhajan, Marc Tremblay, and Ammachi, the Hugging Saint.

Her TV Appearances include *Unsolved Mysteries, Beyond Chance,* and *The Psychic Detectives* as well as several talk shows. Elizabeth has been a guest on hundreds of radio shows, and has her own weekly show *"Let's Find Out",* on OM Media Radio.com – Mondays at 6:00 PM Eastern and 3:00 PM Pacific. Her website is one of the top-rated in her field.

Elizabeth facilitates her own healing classes, using the Divine Seals and Spiritual Chakras from her books; *Ascension—Accessing The Fifth Dimension,* this book, *Backstage,* and the *NEW Spiritual Chakras.* She is located in Warner, NH

Website: *new-visions.com*

Phone: 201-934-8986—24 hour service

E-Mail: Elizabeth_joyce.16@aol.com

CPSIA information can be obtained
at www.ICGtesting.com
Printed in the USA
LVHW080039120121
676256LV00014B/1253